BURIED TREASURE

Also by Ted Schroder

Inward Light

BURIED TREASURE

Recovering The Mysteries of Faith

Ted Schroder

Ted Schroder

Copyright © 2005 Ted Schroder
All Rights Reserved

Library of Congress Control Number
2005900377

ISBN: 0-9748086-1-X

Scripture taken from the HOLY BIBLE, NEW INTERNATIONAL VERSION. Copyright © 1973, 1978, 1984 International Bible Society. Used by permission of Zondervan Bible Publishers.

The Message by Eugene H. Peterson, copyright © 1993, 1994, 1995, 1996, 2000, 2001, 2002. Used by permission of NavPress Publishing Group, All rights reserved.

Quantity discounts are available on bulk purchases of this book for educational, gift purposes, or as premiums for increasing magazine subscriptions or renewals.

Watercolor art by Joann Speas
Dust jacket design by Skip 'N Stones Productions

Amelia Island Publishing, Inc.
P.O. Box 8014
Amelia Island Florida 32035
www.ameliapublishing.com

Printed in the United States of America

THE HID TREASURE

IN THE FIELD of my soul
    there is a treasure hidden.
O my soul, do you not know?
    Have you no desire for it,
    are you seeking?
No human eye can detect it, nor hand handle;
    secret and silent it lies,
        too deep to reach or reckon.
Yet it is THERE, and it is mine:
I have not bought it, nor inherited,
    still less deserved;
        it is Gift.
By Spirit alone can I awake to it,
    by faith alone find,
        only by love possess.

So wake, spirit of mine, to the search!
    Be my faith resolute to find,
        my love strong to hold!
And then, in the field of my soul,
    YOU are there,
        YOU, my Lord and my God:
more bright than light itself,
    over me like a banner,
    under me, a strong rock,
    around me as a house of defense,
    before me, a beckoning star;
but, richest of all, WITHIN,
    my Treasure for ever;
hidden still, yet Life of my life today;
    tomorrow, my open Glory,
        my LORD, my GOD.

Eric Milner-White

Dedicated
To
John Stott
who, as mentor, colleague, and friend, believed in me,
gave me my first opportunity to serve at All Souls,
Langham Place, London, instilled in me a love for truth,
and has remained an inspiration over his long,
productive life.
"Let us praise illustrious men
who were intelligent advisers,
directed people by their advice,
by their understanding of the popular mind,
and by the wise words of their teaching."
Ecclesiasticus 44:1,3,4 (JB)

CONTENTS

Foreword by George H. Gallup, Jr.
Preface   1
Introduction   3

Part One: Seeking the Treasure

1. Doubting Thomas   13

2. Turning Doubt to Good   21

3. Reasonable Doubt   29

4. A Working Definition of Faith   35

5. The Risk of Faith   43

6. Stages of Faith   53

7. Questioning Faith   61

8. Choosing Faith   69

9. The Subjectivity of Faith   77

10. Faith Has Its Reasons   85

11. The Gift of Faith   93

12. Why I Believe in Jesus Christ   101

Part Two: The Treasures of Faith

13. I Believe	113
14. God the Father Almighty	121
15. The Maker of Heaven and Earth	129
16. Jesus Christ	137
17. His Only Son	143
18. Our Lord	149
19. Conceived by the Holy Spirit, Born of the Virgin Mary	155
20. Suffered Under Pontius Pilate	161
21. Crucified, Dead, and Buried	169
22. Descended to Hell	177
23. Rose From The Dead	185
24. Ascended Into Heaven	193
25. Seated At The Right Hand of God	197
26. Come To Judge the Quick and The Dead	203
27. I Believe in the Holy Spirit	209
28. The Holy, Catholic Church	217

29. The Communion of Saints	223
30. The Forgiveness of Sins	229
31. The Resurrection of the Body	235
32. The Life Everlasting	241
Epilogue	249

FOREWORD

This book, about the treasures of knowing Jesus Christ in one's life, is a treasure in itself. Few works I have encountered address so powerfully yet gracefully the spiritual condition of the day. Surveys indicate that many Americans are on a spiritual quest but at the same time are wandering about and confused, caught between a vague "anything goes" spirituality, on the one hand, and assertions of absolute unyielding faith on the other.

The author reminds readers that we are not being unfaithful by having doubts; that an unexamined faith may be a false faith; that faith and reason are not incompatible. Faithful leaders in history have struggled mightily with doubts. St. Augustine, himself, prayed to God, "I believe, help my unbelief." Ted Schroder encourages us to make an educated and prayerful choice about following Jesus, based on the evidence that is available. Too many people, he maintains, do not experience faith in Christ, because they are unwilling to take the risk. We must take the plunge if we are to be in a position to learn the truth.

In part two the author moves from a discussion of the obstacles to faith, to a careful and reverent reading of The Apostles' Creed. Henceforth, many readers will undoubtedly recite the Creed with new eyes and ears. It is the author's heart's desire that we bring all of our cares, concerns, fears, and pains to Jesus Christ for healing. We then invite the Spirit of God into our lives so that we will know the reality of Christ.

We are called to stand with Jesus against the modern tides of secularism, to be counter cultural. In reference to explorers seeking treasure in sunken vessels in the sea, described in his book, Ted Schroder asks why people do not show similar courage and determination in recovering the treasures of faith? If we make similar efforts, he concludes, we will be richly rewarded.

George H. Gallup, Jr.
The George H. Gallup International Institute
Princeton, New Jersey

PREFACE

"My purpose is that they may be encouraged in heart and united in love, so that they may have the full riches of complete understanding, in order that they may know the mystery of God, namely, Christ, in whom are hidden all the treasures of wisdom and knowledge."
(Colossians 2:2,3)

This book is designed to be an aid to someone who would like to consider how and what to believe about the meaning of life, and yet has doubts and questions about faith in God. The first part of the book is the 'how' of faith. How do you go about it? What does faith mean? How does it square with the facts as we know them? How can we have faith in an age that requires scientific proof? How do we distinguish faith from superstition and prejudice? Why do we have doubts? The second part of the book is about the 'what' of faith. It looks at the content of the Christian faith, and what it is that Christians historically and universally have believed. It is my conviction that Christian faith is a treasure waiting to be discovered, or rediscovered, and when found will enrich the finder beyond her wildest dreams.

It is not meant to be the final word, but my word at the moment, for what it is worth. All I ask it that it helps someone to find their way. Soren Kierkegaard, the Danish writer of the nineteenth century, wrote a preface to one of his publications which I would wish for this book.

"Forasmuch as on being published, it started, figuratively speaking, upon a pilgrimage, I let my eye follow it a little while. I saw then how it fared forth along lonely paths or alone upon the highway. After one and another little misunderstanding, when it was deceived by a fleeting likeness, it finally encountered that single individual whom I with joy and gratitude call *my* reader, that single individual whom it seeks, towards whom as it were it stretches out its arms, that single individual who is willing enough to let himself be found, willing enough to encounter it, whether at the instant it finds him happy and confident or 'weary and pensive.' – On the other hand, forasmuch as on being published it remains, literally speaking, perfectly still, without budging from the spot, I let my eye rest upon it a little while. It stood there like an insignificant little blossom hidden in the immense forest, unsought after either for its splendor, or for its scent, or for its nutriment. But then too I saw or thought I saw how the bird which I call *my* reader suddenly sighted it, plunged down upon the wing, plucked it and took it unto itself. And when I had seen this, I saw no more. Copenhagen, May 5, 1843.[1]

May you, single individual, *my* reader, find in these words what you have been looking for, and much, much more – a treasure that you have dreamed you might some day find.

INTRODUCTION

DISCOVERING A TREASURE SHIP

A few miles south of where I live on Amelia Island, Atlantic Marine, on Hecksher Drive in Jacksonville, has made a business of fitting out ships. Located on the St. John's River, it has easy access to the Atlantic Ocean through Mayport. On May 26, 1987, the *Nicor Navigator*, owned and operated by the Columbus-America Discovery Group, slipped its moorings and headed out to test its crane and winch which was essential for towing the Remote Operated Vehicle (ROV) it was using to locate the site of the *S.S. Central America*, which had sunk in a hurricane on September 12, 1857. The equipment failed, and they had to return to Jacksonville for repairs. On May 31, they departed Atlantic Marine a second time for the test site. Once again they had problems and had to return. On June 5, for the third time in ten days, a river pilot took them out from Atlantic Marine to the ocean.

Gary Kinder in his bestseller *Ship of Gold In The Deep Blue Sea*, tells the enthralling story of the loss of the *Central America*, and its eventual discovery in 8,000 feet of water 160 miles off Cape Henry, Norfolk, Virginia, by a group of scientists and investors headed by Tommy

Thompson of Columbus, Ohio. Tommy worked in 1976 for Mel Fisher who, for seven years, tried to find the Spanish treasure ship *Nuestra Senor de Atocha*, which sank off the Florida Keys in a hurricane in 1622. The *Atocha* carried 901 silver bars, 15 tons of ingot copper, 250,000 newly minted silver coins and 161 pieces of gold bullion, plus other rare artifacts, and jewelry. Mel Fisher did not find and recover the treasure until 1987.

Tommy went on to work for the Battelle Memorial Institute which engaged in research for government and private industry. His interest was in deep-ocean mining. While water covered seventy percent of the world's surface, there had been little research done in deep water due to the hazardous environment and the lack of technology. Tommy set his goal on developing the technology to make deep-ocean research and recovery possible. In 1984, he selected the finding and recovery of the *Central America* as the ideal project to work on. He gathered together a group of venture capitalists who invested in the project which promised a 10,000 percent return.

The *Central America* was carrying gold and gold miners returning from the California goldfields. The ship picked up the cargo and passengers after they had transited across the Panama isthmus. The gold shipment was documented at up to $1.6 million in 1857 prices. Probably the passengers carried an equal amount in addition to the manifest. There was also an official secret shipment designed to shore up the faltering economy of New York. It was estimated at six hundred fifty-pound bar boxes, or another thirty thousand pounds of gold.

The potential investors grilled Tommy Thompson on the feasibility of the enterprise. Before they invested their capital they wanted to know the probability of being able to locate the wreck, overcome the legal issues, and secure the gold. Tommy said that it was sixty percent. Many experts they approached said that it couldn't be done. There were too many variables and challenges to locating and recovering at such a depth. Government agencies had spent multi-millions trying to do it to recover submarines, and had limited success. There was a lot of skepticism, and Tommy himself was honest enough to admit his own agnosticism, but he was convinced that the project was possible, despite the risks involved.

Gary Kinder expressed Tommy's attitude, "Don't know if we can find the ship. Think we can, but don't know. Don't know what the site will be like. Think we do, but don't know. Don't know if we have the technology to recover the gold. Think we have, but don't know. We do know the ship sank, that it carried at least three tons of gold, that it rests in about eight thousand feet of water, that no one else has recovered the treasure. And I think I can put together a project to do what no one else has done before: find the remains of a three-hundred-foot, wooden-hulled ship in a stretch of ocean bigger than the state of Rhode Island and go down to the bottom and pluck the treasure from the debris with a robot. Don't know if we can keep the treasure. Think we can, but don't know. Don't know how to market the treasure. We'll figure that out."[1]

I count nine "don't knows" in that paragraph! What faith is required to undertake such a project, and to risk investing thousands of dollars in it? There is no certainty here. There is no proof that this will be successful. Yet many people invested their time and money in it because there was the possibility of gain and glory.

Agnostics will say that they cannot believe in God or Christ because they don't know if he really exists, or they are not sure that Jesus Christ was divine. Yet Tommy Thompson decided to pursue what he didn't know until he did know, and he could be sure. I want to pursue the buried treasure of faith to see how we can be sure that it exists and that we can discover it for ourselves.

The Bible says: "Now faith is being sure of what we hope for and certain of what we do not see."[2]

Tommy could not see the *Central America*, but he was sure going to try and find it. We cannot see God in a physically, scientifically-verifiable form, but faith is the willingness to seek until we find.

Tommy did not find the *Central America* in 1987. The following year he acquired a new ship which he sailed up the St. John's River in Jacksonville, to Green Cove Springs, where it was transformed into the *Arctic Discoverer*. All winter he and his research team had been examining the sonar records for the fourteen hundred square miles searched in 1987. They identified an image which strongly resembled what they were looking for and determined that they would explore that target. More investors had to be attracted to finance this next stage of the project. The original investors kicked in another $1.5 million and new investors added another million dollars.

On August 19, a tug pulled *Arctic Discoverer* from the dock in Green Cove Springs, and towed it to Jacksonville, where it continued to be refitted at a marina near the mouth of the St. John's River for the next week. On August 28, the *Arctic Discoverer* traveled out of its dock through Mayport into the Atlantic. In September, they located the ship, whose remains covered an area of over ten acres.

On October 1, they discovered the treasure. "The bottom was carpeted with gold," said Tommy. "Gold everywhere, like a garden. The more you looked, the more you saw gold growing out of everything, embedded in all the wood and beams. It was amazing, clear back in the far distance bars stacked on the bottom like brownies, bars stacked like loaves of bread, bars that appear to have slid into the corner of a room. Some of the bars formed a bridge, all gold bars spanning one area of treasure over here and another area over here, water underneath, and the decks collapsed through on both sides. Then there was a beam with coins stacked on it, just covered, couldn't see the beam it had so many coins on it."

"So many bricks lay tumbled upon another at myriad angles that the thirty-foot pile appeared to be the remnants of an old building just demolished. Except these were bricks of gold: bricks flat, bricks stacked, bricks upright, bricks cocked on top of other bricks. And coins single, coins stacked, coins once in stacks now collapsed into spreading piles."[3]

One of the largest bars of California gold was 754.95 oz., $14,045 value in 1857. Today in bullion value alone, it could be worth $250,000. James Lamb the coin expert from Christie's said that it was "impossible to describe the significance, the potential monetary value, the general excitement of this find. All of these hitherto extraordinarily rare, desirable artifacts in perfect condition, in huge piles is just... it's beyond my imagination."[4] The total value of the treasure is still undetermined.

It is impossible to completely determine the existence of God, the atoning efficacy of the Cross, the truth of the resurrection of Jesus and its effects on those who believe. Thomas, one of the original twelve disciples of Jesus, doubted until he could see the risen Jesus with his own eyes and touch him with his own hands. Yet Tommy Thompson and his investors, put aside their doubts and were willing to wager millions on being able to find gold. They were willing to take years to seek until they found what they were looking for. What does this say to us about how much we are willing to invest in seeking first the buried treasure of the eternal kingdom of heaven Jesus proclaimed?

The value, if it is real, of what St. Paul described as "the unsearchable riches of Christ"[5], must be worth all the effort, all the giving, all the questioning, all the exploring, all the praying, all the learning, all the serving, all the time, that is required. Not to seek it, and then to find out after death that it was there all the time for us to discover ("The word is near you; it is in your mouth and in your heart, that is, the word of faith we are proclaiming."[6]), would be a terrible omission, a lack of courage, and fill us with eternal regret.

Those who deny the existence of God, and the truth of Christ, persuade many that it is a foolish and unprofitable exercise to seek the certainty that faith brings. But that has always been the counsel of those who dismiss explorers and inventors as people who waste their time chasing up blind alleys. Settling for the immediate and the obvious has never satisfied the human spirit. There always have been those who have pushed the envelope, who have gone where no one has gone before. Years later posterity hails them as the true visionaries who made possible the advances in technology that created the environment in which our civilization has developed. Seeking for faith in Christ is no different from seeking for a truth, if it exists, that can change our world for good. The rewards are worth it: eternal life, heaven, forgiveness, empowerment by God's Spirit, divine love and acceptance, hope, joy, human fulfillment, and ultimate justice, are a few of the treasures to be found.

Gary Kinder closes his remarkable account with these words: "They had proved the experts wrong. You could work on the bottom of the deep ocean, do intricate work carefully and heavy work delicately, and you didn't have to spend hundreds of millions of dollars to do it. You just had to shed old ways of thinking and reexamine old assumptions and do it smart from the beginning. You had to keep diverging, even beyond the point where it all became difficult and confusing. That's where Tommy lives, and he made those around him live there too, some for far longer than is comfortable for most people. Yet just on the other side of that juncture is where impossibility sometimes vanishes and the world can be seen in a new way. ... Historic ship recovery was really an adventure in thinking, a way of looking at the world. Finding the treasure of the *Central America* was a goal, but it wasn't the purpose. The purpose was to unveil the treasures of the deep ocean, to enhance our understanding of history, to advance marine archeology, to further science, to form new corporate cultures, to develop technology. Going after treasure was like plowing and planting a field. Tommy had broached the idea ...back in 1985. 'If you do that,' he said, 'all kinds of things can blossom.'"[7]

These words can provide us with an analogy. The exercise of faith sometimes requires shedding old ways of thinking and re-examining old assumptions. Sometimes we have to get out of our comfort zones. Yet, when we get to the assurance of faith we find that impossibility vanishes, and the world can be seen in a new way. Faith is an adventure in thinking, a way of looking at the world. The purpose of following Christ, and seeing life through his eyes, is to unveil the treasures of, what C.S. Lewis called 'deep heaven', to enhance our understanding of reality, to advance the kingdom of God, and to further the work of Gospel. It is like going after buried treasure.

PART ONE

SEEKING THE TREASURE

We begin the search with trying to understand the nature of faith and what can prevent it. Doubts need to be explored to see whether they pose insurmountable obstacles to faith. Risks need to be weighed, and the various stages of the journey should be anticipated before setting out on the quest. We need some sort of map in order to start. But many people react against having to follow a map. In matters of belief they don't want to have to ask for directions on route. As a result they often get lost.

C.S.Lewis tells the story of a military man who, though he confessed to being religious, had no time for doctrines such as found in the creeds. He preferred his religion to be mysterious and experiential, and did not want to know about the facts of the faith. His experience of God was more real to him than the words conveying the affirmations of the faith.

Lewis said that it was like looking at the Atlantic Ocean, and then looking at a map of the Atlantic Ocean. You turn from looking at real waves to looking at a bit of colored paper. "But here comes the point. The map is admittedly only colored paper, but there are two things you have to remember about it. In the first place, it is based on what hundreds and thousands of people have found out by sailing the real Atlantic. In that way, it has behind it masses of experience just as real as the one you could have from the beach; only, while yours would be a single glimpse, the map fits all those different experiences together. In the second place, if you want to go anywhere, the map is absolutely necessary. [The creeds] are only a kind of map. But that map is based on the experiences of hundreds of people who really were in touch with God. If you want to get any further, you must use the map."

The military officer's religion led him nowhere. "In fact, that is just why a vague religion – all feeling God in nature, and so on – is so attractive. It is all thrills and no work; like watching the waves from the beach. But you will not get to Newfoundland by studying the Atlantic that way, and you will not get eternal life by simply feeling the presence of God in flowers or music. Neither will you get anywhere by looking at maps without going to sea. Nor will you be very safe if you go to sea without a map."[1]

I hope that this book will provide a map you can use to find the buried treasure and to recover it so that you can enjoy it.

1

DOUBTING THOMAS

Tommy Thompson enlisted the help of Bob Evans, who was also a trivia and history buff. They were both drawn to unusual projects and to what Tommy called "thought experiments." They spent hours in animated discussion about inventions, innovation, and exploration. Tommy also consulted with Dr. Lawrence D. Stone, one of the world's leading experts on search theory, a method using probability, and statistical analysis to find objects, particularly in the ocean. Between them they developed a "data correlation matrix" to find the location of the *Central America* on the seabed. They came up with a 1,400-square-mile search area (larger than the state of Rhode Island). Tommy Thompson was a man of vision. Where did it come from? From his earliest years he had been encouraged in his curiosity by his parents. He was raised in an educational and family atmosphere that fostered enquiry. He searched for answers through one project after another in his school years.

Tommy's father was an engineer, and his mother a nutritionist. They were loving and supportive parents who affirmed Tommy in all that he did, and praised him for his efforts to learn. There was a whole lot of affection for one another in the family. Tommy thought his parents were wonderful. High self esteem, nurtured in this natural way, enabled him to consider options and test theories to find out how things worked. "He wanted to take old ideas, turn them inside out, and apply them in new ways; he wanted to suck the world through his senses and exhale a vision."[1]

The other Thomas, one of the twelve disciples of Jesus, was a twin. We don't hear of his twin, and we know nothing about his childhood. But we know that he also, was always asking questions. He never accepted anything without asking for an explanation. That is what got him a few extra lines in the Gospel of John.

It was recorded that on Easter Sunday Jesus appeared to the disciples in the Upper Room. He came and stood among them, spoke with them, and showed them his wounds. We read that the disciples were overjoyed when they saw him. He commissioned them in his service of preaching the Gospel of forgiveness of sins in the power of the Holy Spirit.

But Thomas was not there. Why, we don't know. When they saw him again the other disciples told him what had happened. They gave their first-hand testimony: "We have seen the Lord!" But Thomas was not easily persuaded. He wanted proof. "Unless I see with my own eyes the nail marks in his hand and put my own finger where the nails were, and put my own hand into his side, I will not believe it."[2]

This desire for first-hand verification is perfectly normal. It is especially understandable when extraordinary claims such as these are made. To have seen and spoken with someone who was certifiably dead cries out for some kind of proof. That is why it is so difficult for modern man to believe anything unless he has had direct experience of it. The resurrection of Jesus is no easier to believe today than it was two thousand years ago. Some people find it easier to believe than others. Thomas needed some proof. He was a doubter of so-called miraculous occurrences.

Why was he such a doubter? Why do many people find it difficult to believe the testimony of others, the witness of history, the record of his post-resurrection appearances, the claims of Christ to be God in the flesh, the Lord of all, the conqueror of death and Hades, the authority of Holy Scripture? What causes some people to be congenital doubters?

Did Thomas suffer from existential angst? Philosophers explore the problem of having a fundamental sense of uncertainty about the reality of existence. Doubt and despair can be the result of a basic pessimism about the human condition. Modern atheistic philosophy, that denies any divine purpose, and defines life in terms of a biological determinism, breeds cynicism. Life that is lived on the surface, that seeks to escape boredom and emptiness through material acquisition and pleasure, is prone to perennial doubt. Doubt cannot be always kept at bay by distraction from anxiety that mindless activities afford.

Perhaps Thomas was plagued with troubling questions that he couldn't ignore. Doubts are often rooted deep in the personality. Did Thomas suffer from emotional mood swings: a manic period when faith was strong, and a depressive period when faith was absent? When we feel good, and life is going well, faith is easy. But when we pass through periods of discouragement, doubts resurface. It is important to distinguish mood swings from genuine doubt. Our feelings have to be offered up to God, to be purified, so that we can experience peace. We can choose to be governed by our feelings or by our daily commitment to follow Jesus. Jesus said, "Come to me all you who are weary and burdened, and I will give you rest. Take my yoke [i.e. my teaching] upon you and learn from me, for I am gentle and humble in heart, and you will find rest for your souls. For my yoke is easy and my burden is light." [3]

Was Thomas at a turning point in his development and personal history? Different seasons of our lives affect our faith and our doubts. Changes in life lead to vulnerability which leaves us open to doubt. Transitions, a sense of danger, insecurity, loneliness, which Thomas must have been experiencing, can cause doubt and fear. Adolescence, mid-life crises, menopause, empty nests, illnesses and retirement bring stresses that cause us to doubt. As we age we ask, "Is there nothing more?" and we face the three big D's: decline, depression and death.

Did the death of Jesus trigger some emotional connection in Thomas's life? The loss of Jesus may have led him to contemplate other losses in his life, which he interpreted as abandonment by significant people, and consequent feelings of anger, or lack of value. Some doubts can be traced to painful chapters in our emotional history. Deaths of parents, siblings, or close friends in tragic circumstances, may have left unfinished business. The fact that Jesus had appeared to the other disciples and not him may have upset him. Was Jesus avoiding him? Was he not important? Why was he being put on the spot and expected to believe when the others had it easy? It could have looked to him as favoritism.

Pressure points and crisis events can shape our doubts. Job losses, illness, bereavements, tragedy of one kind or another, may push us to doubt. Loss of children or other people we love, often cause us to doubt that there is a God of love. Perhaps this is what led to Thomas's doubting. He had undergone the stunning shock and stress of Jesus' arrest, trial, torture and execution. This was a major life crisis for Thomas. All his hopes and dreams had crashed and burned.

Parental abuse causes distrust and doubt of any authority figures. "New York University psychology professor Paul Vitz, in his book *Faith of the Fatherless*, studied the childhood of several well-known atheists and saw strong evidence that their rejection of God is directly related to father pain: the death of a father or abuse or abandonment by their fathers. Vitz points out that Friedrich Nietzsche, the philosopher who declared that 'God is dead,' lost his father at age four. Samuel Butler, skeptical British novelist, was often brutally beaten by his 'pious' father. Sigmund Freud said his father was a 'pervert' and built much of his psychological theory around father hatred. Joseph Stalin's father beat him unmercifully. Madelyn Murray O'Hair once tried to kill her father with a butcher knife. Vitz suggests that after studying these and other 'major historical rejecters of God …. We find a weak, dead or abusive father in every case.' Consequently Vitz urges great compassion for atheists, because behind their unbelief, in all likelihood lies some painful memory. So as you examine your doubts, you may want to honestly confront the possibility that one of your roadblocks to faith may be some pain from the past."[4]

Dr. Lynn Anderson, president of Hope Network, claims that the pace of our lives breeds doubts. He calls it *cognitive overload*.[5] The impact of the media upon us transforms every day into a crisis as we absorb the tragic events in the world through our television screens. We are *overstimulated* by our environment and *overcommitted* in our schedule. We keep ourselves busy so that we do not have to find time for reflecting and listening. Activism, no matter how well-intentioned, leaves life shallow. It can also leave us with faith that may appear to be a mile wide but may not be an inch deep. Cynicism and skepticism pours over us from the talking heads, and the experts. As in the garden of Eden, the tempter can stimulate these roots of doubt and encourage their growth so that we question the presence of God. The influence of evil seems more pervasive than the power of the goodness of God when we see innocent civilians and children killed or maimed by terrorists. "Where is God in all of that carnage?" we ask.

Henri Nouwen refers to this experience as 'the absence of God'. But some of the times when God seems to be absent may actually be fulfilling his purpose. "His absence... is often so deeply felt that it leads to a new sense of His presence."[6] When we feel that God is absent, he may be more completely and sharply focused in our conscious thoughts, more so than when we take for granted that he is very near. Nouwen writes,
"The mystery of God's presence, therefore, can be touched only by a deep awareness of his absence. It is in the center of our longing for the absent God that we discover his footprints... In the patient waiting for the loved one, we discover how much he has filled our lives already. Just as the love of a mother for her son can grow deeper when he is far away, just as children can learn to appreciate their parents more when they have left the home, just as lovers can rediscover each other during long periods of absence, so our intimate relationship with God can become deeper and more mature by the purifying experience of his absence."[7]

When you consider your doubts, look for its roots in your basic temperament, or your particular stage in life, or to a negative experience either long past or recent. Doubt may have more to do with your personality or your personal history than it does with the facts, with the issue of truth, or the conflict between faith and knowledge.

Who knows what were the roots of Thomas's doubts about the resurrection? Eventually he came to believe. Some of us take longer to process the information we need in order to experience the presence of Christ. That does not mean that we should give up or summarily reject the evidence we have in hand. It means that we need to be patient and humble enough to be open to what God might want to teach us.

A week later, the next Sunday, the first day of the week, the Lord's day, when the disciples were gathered together again (the second Sunday in the Christian era), Jesus came and stood among them, as he does whenever his church gathers. He said to Thomas, "Put your finger here; see my hands. Reach out your hand and put it into my side. Stop doubting and believe." When Thomas saw Jesus he acknowledged him with words of personal faith, "My Lord and my God."

Then Jesus told him, "Because you have seen me, you have believed; blessed are those who have not seen and yet have believed." [8]

Jesus says to every one, "Stop doubting and believe." That means making a choice. Will I consciously believe, or will I choose to continue to doubt? Doubt is a decision, just as much as faith. Feelings of uncertainty or doubt, should not prevent me from making the decision to believe in Jesus and to follow him. Sometimes I have to act on my choices before the feelings will follow. The habit of keeping company with Jesus, will result in a secure relationship of love, which fosters faith. Walking in the way of Christ each day, can gradually dispel doubt, until it withers away through lack of attention. Faith needs to be fed, and doubt needs to be starved, through prayer, study, service, witness, and worship. In that way the past can be put behind me, and the future becomes an adventure of faith, with all the possibilities the kingdom of God promises. It is the only way to live.

2

TURNING DOUBT TO GOOD

Doubt is a double-edged sword. It can act as either a deterrent or a stimulant. Doubt about whether it was possible to sail west across the Atlantic Ocean could have kept Christopher Columbus from discovering America. Instead, he doubted that the world was flat and that he would fall off the edge if he traveled too far. He used his doubt to spur him on to new endeavor. Doubt, may in fact, help us to recover our faith. Doubt which persists may prove to be of some value. This was the case of a man who gave us a case study of how belief and doubt could co-exist and produced a prayer that has echoed in the hearts of countless others since.

There is nothing worse than having to experience the suffering of your child. A father brought his son to the disciples in the hope that the boy would be healed, but they could not help him. This man is like so many parents today who helplessly watch their child suffering from some malignant disease, caught in the grip of some addiction, or going off the rails by living at the mercy of their peer group. Such parents don't know where to turn for help. Sometimes all that they can do is to bring them to Jesus in their prayers. The disciples brought this boy to Jesus who, when asked by the father, "if you can do anything, take pity on us and help us." Jesus replied by raising his eyebrows and challenging the father, "If I can? Everything is possible for him who believes." What an extraordinary claim! It challenges us today: the extreme possibility of faith. Yet we know that the possibility of healing is not easy. We cannot say to others, "Just have faith." This is why the boy's father cries out in his desperation, "I do believe, help me overcome my unbelief!"[1]

He has a faith that struggles with doubt. He is honest about the struggle he experiences. He pleads for help just as he is, a doubter. The father does not come to Jesus with a demand but with humility. He does not try to fake a faith he doesn't possess. He pleads with Jesus to do what he can. Yet Jesus honors the man who would bring his son out of compassion to seek help. The prayer of the father is the prayer I can own for myself: "I believe, help my unbelief."

Many of us struggle with doubt even though we have faith and want to believe. For many people pure faith is difficult because of the damage done them in childhood or in the trauma of life. Doubt may have its roots in our basic temperament, or our particular stage in life. Doubt and faith co-exist for many. Yet that may be more normal than you imagine. In fact, there may be a value in experiencing doubt – or unbelief.

Gary E. Parker has written about this in his book, *The Gift of Doubt: From crisis to authentic faith*. He claims that doubt can do us good, that doubt is not always evil, and that doubt can help us to have a stronger faith. "If we maintain an openness to new truth, ...we might find that uncertainty can actually enliven and strengthen our faith. Dr. Clark Pinnock proposes, 'There is also a good side to this sort of uncertainty... Doubt can spur deeper reflection and further discovery.... Doubting may lead to greater certainty."²

Gary Parker suggests four ways doubt can be turned to good. First of all, doubt can test the truth of faith. Thomas Gutherie wrote, "Are not many damned just because they never doubt? They go on, satisfied with themselves; not doubting but that they are on the right course, when every step they take leads them further and further astray."³

An unexamined faith may be a false faith. Much of Jesus' criticism of the Pharisees centered on their dogmatic arrogance. They had their minds made up and were not open to other interpretations of the truth. Fanatical adherence to religious conviction is not necessarily a virtue. When the mind is closed to other truth, there is bred in the believer an intolerance and a cruelty that is incompatible with a God of love.

When you go on a long journey in your own vehicle, you don't assume that the automobile is in good order. You have it checked and serviced for you don't want it to break down on the journey and inconvenience you. Doubt serves as a testing ingredient of faith. It subjects our beliefs to trials to see if those beliefs have the power necessary to complete an arduous journey. A faith that is worthwhile is a faith that is checked for weakness. Doubt provides that check. To be never in doubt is to invite disaster.

Second, doubt destroys faith that doesn't deserve our continued allegiance. A naïve trust in something or someone who doesn't deserve it is destructive. People learn that too much faith in corrupt political leaders, or unfaithful spouses, or fair-weather friends leads to disappointment. Thinking the best of someone, who continually lets you down and doesn't follow through on promises, is unhealthy. To continue to believe in something that has proved itself unworthy of our faith shows our credulity rather than our common sense.

By 1530, Copernicus had questioned the accepted belief of astronomy that the earth was the center of the known universe. He put forward the theory that the sun was actually at the center and that the earth and the other planets revolved around it. The church rejected his theory, but future discoveries proved him correct. We know what happened to Galileo. Their doubts about current beliefs destroyed faith in a system that did not deserve continued support, and established a new truth valuable to human life.

Any doubt that destroys faith in any false god is good, and serves God's purpose. When doubt upends a false faith, it serves as an asset to a true one. The faith that cannot survive the trials and tests of life probably didn't deserve to live anyway.

Third, doubt enhances a faith that proves itself worthy of commitment. Doubt takes faith and exercises it so that it cannot help but grow stronger. If faith never encounters doubt, if truth never struggles with error, if good never battles with evil, how can faith know its own power? How can it enhance its power if it never exercises its perception? A faith that struggles with doubt becomes strong through that struggle.

Robert Schuller tells the story of a tornado that destroyed his family farm buildings. In half an hour nine freshly painted buildings were completely obliterated. Twenty-six years of hard labor had been wiped out. "Dad got out of the car, ordering us to wait, and walked with his cane around the clean-swept, tornado-vacuumed farmyard." Doubts, I'm sure arose in his mind. "Why did

God allow this to happen? Haven't I served God faithfully? Doesn't God care about me and my welfare? If God is real, why didn't he stop this tornado?" As he picked through the trash, he found a piece of molded plaster that had hung on the kitchen wall. The motto said, "Keep looking to Jesus." So, Schuller wrote, his Dad didn't quit. With God on his side and, 'looking to Jesus', he could start over. And he did just that.[4]

The faith of Schuller's family stood a stern test that day and it survived. Without question, nothing could have tested their faith any stronger. Their faith gained strength because it had looked into the face of destruction and had not blinked.

Rufus Jones, the Quaker pastor and teacher in Maine once wrote, "A twice-born faith, a rebuilt faith, is superior to an inherited faith that has never stood the strain of a great testing storm. If you have not clung to a broken piece of your old ship in the dark night of the soul, your faith may not have the sustaining power to carry you through to the end of the journey."[5]

Fourth, doubt forces us to find reasons for our faith. Many deny that doubt has any value. Herbert Williams, in his book, *No Room for Doubt*, sums up this viewpoint. "Doubting can serve no useful purpose whatever, as it provides nothing we need in the challenging quest for answers. Doubt... is a negative attitude which cannot accomplish in the interest of positive inquiry into problems that are real, pressing, and ever-present."[6]

This kind of attitude flies in the face of the biblical approach where the apostles argued, debated, and discussed, with people of many faiths, in order to prove the validity of their claims. We cannot expect people to listen to our beliefs if we cannot explain the reasons for our faith. St. Peter wrote, "Always be prepared to give an answer to everyone who asks you to give the reason for the hope you have. But do this with gentleness and respect." [7]

Doubt forces us to express our belief in coherent and rational statements. Doubt makes us deal honestly with the troublesome issues of life. Faith does not require us to bury our heads in the sand lest we be disturbed. True faith will enable us to look difficulties in the eye, and respond with integrity to the truth we know. If you struggle with misgivings and uncertainties, do not be forced by a false sense of Christian piety to hide your doubts. Faithful men and women in history have struggled greatly with the fire of doubt burning within them.

"Like a fire that burns away the underbrush so new trees can reach new heights, our doubts can help us achieve a faith that grows stronger and reigns supreme in spite of the uncertainties we often face."[8]

I don't believe everything people tell me. The world is filled with people trying to sell me something that will benefit them rather than me. Too many people are ripped off by con artists. If something is too good to be true it usually is. Doubt in these cases is very valuable. It may prevent you from losing your shirt. It is healthy to question the claims of others. Doubt can be very reasonable.

In the mean time, we return to the father who prayed, *"I believe, help my unbelief."* His son was healed. What happened to his faith? What needs to happen to us that will bring us to seek help from Jesus? What is possible for us if we believe?

Perhaps you need to make this man's prayer your own, and bring all your cares, concerns, fears and pains to him for healing. When you do so you will discover that "all things are possible to him who believes." Prayer changes things. As Jesus said, "This kind [the evil spirit in the boy] can come out only by prayer." We may try everything else in life, but prayer is our first and last resort. Our need, faith, and our doubt drives us to seek for help. When we do we discover that the Savior is there to heal.

3

REASONABLE DOUBT

The book of Ecclesiastes in the Bible expresses the skepticism of a life that has seen most things, and finds it hard to make sense of it all. The more we know about life, the more cynical we can become. We may have more, rather than less, unanswered questions as we age. We may find that religious faith, and personal trust in others, is harder rather than easier to come by. A friend who had experienced a great deal of betrayal and disappointment by people whom he expected more of, shared with me that his wife had taken it "all rather badly as it stings and hurts, and she doesn't trust anyone just now." There are plenty of reasons to doubt that there is a good and loving God if we look for them. Some of us may want to have a stronger faith but the advice people may give us may become reasons to doubt.

Lynn Anderson in *If I Really Believe, Why Do I Have These Doubts?*[1] lists several reasons to doubt, several blind alleys seekers are encouraged to explore that lead them nowhere but to frustration.

First, is the advice that faith requires you to turn off your mind, and to just try harder to believe. "Don't think about it – just believe!" Wanting to believe, or wishful thinking. does not make it so. Trying to ignore troublesome doubts, and attempting to sweep them under the rug, will not work. We fool ourselves if we try to believe by being intellectually dishonest. Closing our eyes to problems will not make them go away. God made our minds so that we can interpret what is happening in life. We are created to think through our understanding of life. That is why we have a book like Ecclesiastes in the Bible. It is the journal of an intelligent seeker who is struggling with trying to make sense of the issues of life. His words 'are like goads, his collected sayings like firmly embedded nails – given by one Shepherd'(12:11). They are meant to goad us to action in our search for answers. When difficulties arise in life, we cannot dismiss them as though they do not matter. We must think through their implications and find a resolution of them in our beliefs. To be a Christian is not to commit intellectual suicide as some people contend, even if some Christians behave that way.

John Stott wrote a little book entitled, *Your Mind Matters*,[2] in which he criticized "the misery and menace of mindless Christianity." He argues why it is important that we use our minds. "Faith is not credulity. H.L. Mencken...once said that 'faith may be defined briefly as an illogical belief in the occurrence of the improbable.' But Mencken was wrong. Faith is not credulity. To be credulous is to be gullible, to be entirely uncritical, undiscerning and even unreasonable in one's beliefs. But it is a great mistake to suppose that faith and reason are incompatible."[3] He quotes Proverbs 2:3-6

"if you call out for insight
and cry aloud for understanding,
and if you look for it as silver
and search for it as for hidden treasure,
then you will understand the fear of the Lord

and find the knowledge of God.
For the Lord gives wisdom,
and from his mouth come
knowledge and understanding."

The second reason to doubt is to assume that faith is like something you can catch. To this way of thinking all you have to do is to wait for faith to happen. It will be like waiting for lightning to strike, like it did Saul on the Damascus road.

Parents who take this approach do not influence their children in any direction. They say that their children will make up their own minds when they grow up. Others say that the doubts their children experience will go away when they mature. I heard my aunt and uncle say that about their children. It was an excuse for them not going to church. As a result they deprived their children of the advantages of a childhood Christian education. They have had a hard time in adult life catching up.

More education or maturation does not necessarily bring faith. Faith is our response to revelation, and requires a choice on our part. Many people have reason to doubt because they believe that they have to do nothing and God has to do everything. God calls us to choose. "Choose you this day, whom you will serve."[4] Soren Kierkegaard calls the refusal to choose, to make a decision of faith, cowardice. "Cowardice wants to prevent the step of making a decision. To accomplish this it takes to itself a host of glorious names. In the name of caution cowardice abhors any over-hastiness. It is against doing anything before the time is ripe.... In the end, failure to decide prevents one from doing what is good."

The third reason to doubt is the attitude that faith requires definitive proof. To this way of thinking, conclusive proof in the form of rational arguments is essential to faith. Since such proof is lacking, faith is, what Mark Twain defined as, "believing what any fool knows ain't so." But no person can be forced to believe by logic. Faith does not come to a person by being argued into it. If this were so, the smarter people would be the first to believe, and the duller people the last. But the opposite may be true. Paul, who, despite doing a lot of arguing himself, quoted Isaiah 29:14

" 'I will destroy the wisdom of the wise; the intelligence of the intelligent I will frustrate.' Where is the wise man? Where is the scholar? Where is the philosopher of this age? Has not God made foolish the wisdom of the world."[5]

Intelligence levels have little to do with faith. You cannot reach a conclusion about faith in Christ based upon proof beyond a reasonable doubt. Faith requires a risk, a leap, or it would not be faith. It is a decision without complete proof and leaves a lot of questions unanswered. Faith is a leap based not on proof but trust in the evidence that is available.

There is no life without this kind of trust. We decide what is worthy of our trust without requiring absolute proof. We trust ourselves to all sorts of people, machinery and organizations because we have enough evidence that they are worthy of our trust. We do not completely understand many things we trust every day, e.g. banks, automobiles, airplanes, telephones, computers. But because we have evidence that they work, we use them, act on them, put our trust in them. We are called to examine, not proofs for the existence of

God, but evidence of a loving relationship with the personal God. Frederick Buechner writes,

"We all want to be certain, we all want proof, but the kind of proof that we tend to want – scientifically or philosophically demonstrable proof that would silence all doubts once and for all – would not, in the long run, I think, answer the fearful depths of our need at all. For what we need to know, of course, is not just that God exists, not just that beyond the steely brightness of the stars there is a cosmic intelligence of some kind to keep the whole show going, but that there is a God right here in the thick of our day-to-day lives who might not be writing messages about himself in the stars but who in one way or another is trying to get messages through our blindness as we move around here knee-deep in the fragrant muck and misery and marvel of the world. It is not objective proof of God's existence that we want but, whether we use religious language for it or not, the experience of God's presence. That is the miracle we are really after."[6]

The fourth reason to doubt is the belief that faith comes through miracles. If only we could see a miracle happening! Would we believe? Witnessing miracles does not automatically generate faith. Take the Pharisees for example. "Even after Jesus had done all these miraculous signs in their presence they still would not believe in him.....For this reason they *could not* believe."[7] Lynn Anderson comments on St. John's conclusion:

"What an ominous statement. Notice that the unbelief of the people John was describing was a *choice*. Faith in Jesus would have threatened their vested interests. Consciously or unconsciously, they had chosen to set their hearts against Christ and had continued choosing not to believe in spite of miraculous proof over a long period of time. Finally, their hearts so hardened that even the miraculous signs of Jesus himself would not touch them! It is possible to reject faith so often that we can wind up actually dismantling our believing machinery.

The mightiest signs and wonders cannot change our hearts! Only the Spirit of God can do that! Through the gospel, the Spirit of God can move us to choose faith. But even then, he will not force us – only touch us, convict us, call us on. How we respond is entirely up to us."[8]

If you ask people who do not believe in Christ, what it would take for them to believe they usually mention one of these reasons to doubt. They want a miracle, or conclusive proof, or they want to wait for divine intervention, or they or their peer group think that faith is anti-intellectual. These reasons, I believe, are ill-founded.

There are plenty of reasons to doubt. We can always find a reason to avoid believing in God and serving him. The choice is ours. But God sent his Son so that we might believe. We have to decide whether we are going to worship him or not. Examine the evidence, by all means. Faith can be commitment based on the evidence. Our mind is engaged. But at the end of the day you still have to take a leap of faith if you want to experience God's presence. Invite the Spirit of God into your life so that you will know the reality of Christ.

4

A WORKING DEFINITION OF FAITH

In 1986, my wife Antoinette and I were in a shopping mall in Christchurch, New Zealand, when we noticed people looking at the televisions in the stores. My cousin, whom we were meeting for lunch, arrived, and said, "Have you heard about the space shuttle?" We hadn't heard that the *Challenger* had blown up when it took off from the Kennedy Space Center. The horrifying picture that exploded across the screens that day reminded us of the dangers of space exploration. Seven astronauts died that day. On October 7, 1988, after a two and a half year hiatus from space, NASA launched the *Discovery*. Five more astronauts put their lives on the line to try again. They put their faith in the engineers to correct the problems and design a better and safer system. They couldn't know with certainty that they would survive the flight. They couldn't know with perfect confidence that everything would function properly. But they volunteered to go anyway.

Gary Parker, sees in this story a parable of the way faith works in our lives.[1] He finds three elements at work. First, these five crewmen climbed on board the *Discovery* at great personal *risk*. Second, they responded to the call of their mission out of a deep sense of *commitment* to the program of space exploration. Third, their commitment spurred them to *action*. They placed faith in their mission, their ship, their abilities, and their equipment.

==Faith can be defined as the willingness to trust our lives to a person or God, whom we cannot prove as trustworthy,== before the actual moment of risk, commitment and action occurs. We may believe that God, by definition, is trustworthy. "Here is a trustworthy saying: if we are faithless, he will remain faithful, for he cannot disown himself."[2] Faithfulness, or trustworthiness is central to the character of God as revealed in the Scriptures. But having faith, means acting without final knowledge, or proven certainty. It means we *go* before we *know* the final results.

When we define faith in religious terms, it means the same thing. But instead of trusting a mechanical ship, or a crew of support engineers, or even our own abilities, we cast our dependence upon God. Religious faith leads us to take hold of a scientifically unprovable God, and it allows him to take hold of us.

This is what Hebrews 11 is asserting. "Now faith is being certain of what we hope for and certain of what we do not see. This is what the ancients were commended for. By faith we understand that the universe was formed at God's command, so that what is seen was not made out of what was visible."[3]

This is not the same as the description of faith by Ambrose Bierce in his Devil's Dictionary: "belief without evidence in what is told by one who speaks without knowledge of things without parallel."

What is the certainty claimed by faith? *It is the subjective, personal appropriation of the truth that compels us to respond by virtue of its innate authority that meets our own need.* It is not fantasy, the projection of our own desires, as Freud contended "The very idea of 'an idealized Superman' in the sky – to use Freud's phrase – is ' so patently infantile and so foreign in reality, that ... it is painful to think that the great majority of mortals will never rise above this view of life.' He predicted, however, that as the masses of people become more educated, they would 'turn away' from 'the fairy tales of religion.'"[4]

It is not insanity, a delusional obsession with fanatical imaginings, e.g. the portrayal of some preachers and prophets in novels and movies. *The certainty of faith is the willingness to risk our lives for what we consider to be worthwhile, by committing ourselves to something greater than ourselves, and taking appropriate action to do something about it.* We are not talking about intellectual faith in abstract theory, but the faith that causes us to do something different with our lives.

If you review the names of the ancient heroes and heroines of faith listed in Hebrews 11, you will find that their faith resulted in risk, commitment and action based on their trust in the guiding hand of God.

People can have this sort of faith without being religious. Marxists and capitalists place their faith in a political and economic system, which they believe will provide the greatest benefits for the largest number of people. Materialists place their faith in the proposition that happiness comes through the acquisition of wealth and property and spend their lives trying to prove that it is true.

Pascal (1623-1662) put forward the proposition that faith was a wager. Christianity cannot be proved conclusively by reason, but neither can it be disproved. If it turns out that Christianity is true, we have everything to gain; but if it turns out to be false, we have nothing to lose. We should accept the inevitable risk of faith, and gamble on the truth of Christianity. This was the essential step of Pascal: that doubt leads to faith. "You must wager. It is not optional. You are embarked. Which will you choose then?" We all wager one way or another. Not to acknowledge the wager is to take the risk of losing.

Soren Kierkegaard maintained that "To gain eternity without risking anything is impossible.. 'To risk everything on an 'if', you say. My friend, if you do not take a risk on an 'if', then you take no risk: take away the 'if' and you take away the risk. You cannot really have any objection to risking on an 'if', for this is what risking is. If therefore you have any objection, then it must be against risking itself. Take care that you are not disappointed, by claiming that you have nothing against risking, you are quite ready for that — only not on an 'if', which is just as though one were to say, 'I have nothing against swimming, on the contrary I should love to swim — only not in water.'

"So a shudder seizes the man, and he reaches out to grasp the others: I must have some certainty before I take the risk, he says. Again, to be certain before one takes the risk is putting the cart before the horse, or filling your mouth with flour before you speak. No, if your mouth is full of flour, you must first get rid of it before you can speak. And so with taking a risk. If a man is certain about something, then there is no risk, if he is to take a risk he must get rid of the certainty, as one who as a child was certain, or thought he was, must get rid of the certainty in order to be able to take a risk — so far is it from being true that you must first be certain before you can take a risk.... This is the cunning of existence: the utmost human certainty is just what fools us most certainly for eternity – and the very least human certainty is just what provides the possibility of eternity."[5]

In Robert Frost's *The Road Not Taken*, the poet lamented the necessity of choosing one road over another. He could not take them both, so he took the one less traveled. He describes for us the necessity of commitment, risk and action in selecting one path or another. How do we choose which road to take? Our choice involves the risk of faith.

That does not mean making choices without reference to the realities of our circumstances. We don't choose vocations for which we have no aptitude. We don't make investments when we have no capital. We don't follow gurus whose character is suspect. When we hear a voice calling us to take risks, to take action, to make a commitment, we need to test its validity – to test the spirits to see whether they are from God. We test them by the teaching of Scripture, by the counsel of people we respect, by the inner testimony of the Holy Spirit, and our conscience. But when we have completed this process, and we believe that it is a genuine summons of God to us, then we dare not fail to act upon it.

I am a Christian because I believe for a fact that God came into our world through a particular human being at a particular point in history, and invited me to follow him. I had to make a decision to respond to that call. I had to take the risk that Jesus was real and not a fantasy figure. In my reading of the Gospels I was impressed by who he was, what he did, and said, and claimed to be. I agreed in my mind with the substance of his teaching. But I also had to make a commitment to do something about it. I had to decide to act on what I believed to be true. Would I let him into my life as Lord and Savior? Would I trust in his sacrifice upon the Cross as atonement for my sins? When I did, it began to change my life. I began to find that, because Jesus was God the Son, he was not a mere figure of history but a living presence. Each day he talked with me through his Word and Spirit, and invited my response through prayer. No matter where I was, he was present to assist me and accompany me in all that I did. I was never alone. He brought into my life a purpose, a joy, and a peace that I wanted to share with others.

Decisions regarding my future began to change. Up to this point I was planning to go to university and study law, and then go into politics. Now I wanted to share what I had learned and experienced. Just as those who aspired to become astronauts had to go through a specialized rigorous training, I chose a course of study that would launch me into a different kind of orbit. As my college days were coming to an end, I had to decide which seminary to attend. As I prayed about it, I sought information from seminaries in New Zealand, Australia, the USA and England. Since I was an Anglican, I thought I might as well go to England. If I had been a Roman Catholic, I probably would have chosen to go to Rome. If you were going to do it, I thought, you might as well do it properly, and go to the best school.

Can you see the implications of this definition of faith? "Now faith is being sure of what we hope for and certain of what we do not see." I was risking a lot by leaving home, making a commitment to go overseas, and to take the actions necessary to make it possible. Yet, all this I did as a twenty three year old. It wasn't because I had extraordinary faith, but because I was sure that God was leading me, and certain that he would take care of me to fulfill his purposes. Remember what I said before.

The certainty claimed by faith is the subjective personal appropriation of the truth that compels us to respond by virtue of its innate authority, that meets my own need. I had accepted Jesus' authority in my life, and that liberated me from other desires. Faith is not fantasy, the projection of our own desires. Faith is not insanity, a delusional obsession with fanatical imaginings. *Faith is the willingness to risk our lives for what we consider to be worthwhile, by committing ourselves to something greater than ourselves, and taking appropriate action to do something about it.*

My faith led me to make decisions, and to take actions that literally made me into the person that I now am. My journey to England resulted in my working in London and meeting Antoinette. Our marriage required faith. We took the risk, that though we came from different backgrounds, we were committed to Christ, and to one another, and we took the action that our love required.

When I made the decision to leave New Zealand and go overseas for my graduate education, I had no proof of the validity of my choice. I had no conclusive evidence that God directed me in it. I may believe retrospectively that he did, but I have no conclusive proof. That is why doubt continually plagues us. Without proof, we always have the uncertainty. There is always the possibility that I could have, should have, stayed in New Zealand, and my life would have been very different. But if we possessed proof, then it would no longer be faith, but knowledge.

Clark Pinnock writes, "Faith does not involve a rash decision made without reflection. It is the act of wholehearted trust in the goodness and promises of God who confronts us with his reality and gives us ample reason to believe that he is there."[6]

What about you? What is Christ calling you to do? Too many people do not experience the benefits of faith in Christ because they are not willing to take the risk, to make the commitment that leads to action. They hold back, they compromise, they delay doing anything, and they miss out on the excitement of faith that could launch them into the discovery of new life. Remember Robert Frost's famous lines:

"I took the one less traveled by,
And that has made all the difference."

5

THE RISK OF FAITH

Jon Guttman, in his Editorial for the June, 2002 edition of *Military History*, wrote about three decisive battles that owed their outcomes to calculated risk-taking. He says that officers today are taught risk assessment – the art of comparing the importance of one's mission against the risks involved. There is actually a matrix that can be used to calculate the relative likelihood and severity of the risk, enabling the leader to determine what can be done to reduce those risks. The risk must always be calculated against the reward. There is a difference between a reckless risk and a calculated risk, and a commander who is skilled at the latter will invariably accomplish more than one who will not accept risk at all.

He cited the calculated risk taken 60 years ago by Japanese Admiral Yamamoto. Desperate to draw the U.S. Navy's aircraft carrier force into a decisive battle, Yamamoto launched a diversionary carrier strike against Dutch Harbor, Alaska, and invaded Attu and Kiska in the Aleutian Islands, at the same time that he dispatched the Combined Fleet to Midway atoll in the Central Pacific. The complicated stratagem was meant to compel the Americans to divide their carrier force, allowing

Yamamoto's main force to annihilate those that tried to defend Midway. But it was undone by the Americans having cracked Japanese codes and learning his true intentions.

Aided by that knowledge, Admiral Chester Nimitz took a calculated risk of his own, sending all three of his remaining first-line fleet carriers to confront the Combined Fleet's four carriers at Midway. The course of the battle that followed highlighted just how much of a risk Nimitz took of losing everything. But the final outcome certainly justified that risk. In exchange for the loss of the carrier *Yorktown*, the Americans sank all four of their principal opponents. Yamamoto got the decisive battle he had sought, but without the outcome he had desired, as the Japanese navy retired from its first major defeat in 350 years.

What risks would you be willing to take to win in the battle of life? The patriarch Abraham took enormous risks in his life. Hebrews 11:8-19 records that when God called him to leave his home, and his country, and his family, he went, even though he did not know where he was going. He went, we are told, by faith. Faith here is characterized as risk-taking.

Abraham is held up as the father of us all by faith. St. Paul writes: "He is the father of us all. As it is written: 'I have made you the father of many nations.' He is our father in the sight of God, in whom he believed – the God who gives life to the dead and calls things that are not as though they were. Against all hope, Abraham in hope believed and so became the ruler of many nations."[1]

Soren Kierkegaard writes, "Surely Christianity's intention is that a person use this life to venture out, to do so in such a way that God can get hold of him, and that one gets to see whether or not he actually has faith."

Often the issues of doubt and faith are described in terms of the intellectual questions people have about God, and life. But, maybe the more difficult questions have to do with whether we are willing to venture out, to risk, to let God get hold of us, to see whether or not we actually have faith. There are many people who profess to believe in God and to follow Christ who have no faith in this sense. They are armchair Christians, who talk the language of Christianity but do precious little about it. Kierkegaard again, "Truth exists for a particular individual only as he himself produces it in action. If the individual prevents the truth from being for him in that way, we have a phenomenon of the demonic. Truth has always had many loud proclaimers, but the question is whether a person will in the deepest sense acknowledge the truth, allow it to permeate his whole being, accept all its consequences, and not have an emergency hiding place for himself and a Judas kiss for the consequences."

Abraham did not have the Bible. He did not have a church. He lived in a pagan society. Archeologists have discovered that that Ur of the Chaldees, located on the Euphrates River in what is today southern Iraq, nineteen hundred years BC, boasted an elaborate system of writing, sophisticated mathematical calculations, educational facilities, and extensive business and religious records. They worshipped Nammu the moon-god. The royal cemetery reveals that ritual burials were sealed with the horrors of human sacrifice. Abraham worshipped these pagan gods.[2] At this point in human history "the world was lost in degrading views of God. From the bull-worship of Crete, to the animal deities of brilliant Egypt, from the worship of the Sun-god on the

Phoenician coast, to the sadistic and sensual deities of which the sailors who traded to the Indus and the Malabar coast could tell, it was one wide story of burdensome corruption. Some search for something purer, better, holier must have stirred in the heart of Abraham of Ur,"[3] because the Most High God appeared to him and called him out of his native land to go, he knew not where. And he went! What kind of risk was he taking to do that? What motivated him to pull up the stakes of his tent, leave his known world for the unknown, and go on the road? What sort of reward was he anticipating? God made him some promises which made his journey and dislocation worthwhile.

"The Lord said to Abram, 'Leave your country, your people and your father's household and go to the land I will show you. I will make you into a great nation and I will bless you; I will make your name great, and you will be a blessing. I will bless those who bless you, and whoever curses you I will curse; and all peoples on earth will be blessed through you.'"[4]

He made his home in the promised land like a stranger in a foreign country. He looked forward to the city that was to come, whose architect and builder is God. He saw his life in this world as a journey where nothing was permanent. He did not put roots down where he lived because he had invested in the future.

God told him that he was to have offspring as numerous as the stars in the heavens, but no children were born to him and Sarah. Then the Lord told him that his wife was to have a child in her old age. Abraham thought it was so funny that he fell facedown and laughed about the absurdity of it.[5]

St. Paul comments: "Without weakening in his faith, he faced the fact that his body was as good as dead

— since he was about a hundred years old — and that Sarah's womb was also dead. Yet he did not waver through unbelief regarding the promise of God, but was strengthened in his faith and gave glory to God, being fully persuaded that God had power to do what he had promised."[6]

When the child does indeed come and grows into a boy, God tells him to go and sacrifice him as a burnt offering on Mount Moriah, and Abraham, saddled up his donkey, and set out to do it. How could he do it? Abraham took the calculated risk that God, who gave him Isaac, when his and Sarah's bodies were past bearing children, could also raise the dead if he were sacrificed.

Kierkegaard calls Abraham the knight of faith, for he is willing to do what is absurd, to take the ultimate of risks in obedience to God. "He who walks the narrow road of faith has no one to advise him — no one understands him. Faith is a marvel, and yet no human being is excluded from it; for that which unites all human life is passion, and faith is a passion."

Did Abraham know all the answers to the questions about God and life? No, of course not. He laughed when God said that he would have a son. He must have doubted at times. But he was passionate in his willingness to take the risk of faith. It was a calculated risk to him because he believed that he could trust the God who called him to venture out in his life.

Miguel de Unamuno wrote, "Those who believe that they believe in God, but without passion in their hearts, without anguish of mind, without uncertainty, without doubt, without an element of despair even in their consolation, believe only in the God idea, not God himself." Faith that never doubts is a dead faith because it is never exercised.

Abraham did not receive what was promised in his own lifetime. "They saw them and welcomed them from a distance.... Instead, they were longing for a better country – a heavenly one."[7] He took the calculated risk that God would deliver on his promises.

Kierkegaard: "Again without risk, no faith; the more risk, the more faith... The absurd is that eternal truth has come into existence in time, that God has come into existence, has been born, has grown up, has come into existence exactly as an individual human being, indistinguishable from any other human being.... Christianity claims to be the eternal, essential truth that has come into existence in time. It proclaims itself as *the* paradox and thus requires the inwardness of faith – that which is an offense to the Jews, foolishness to the Greeks, and an absurdity to the understanding... To know a creed by rote is, quite simply, paganism. This is because Christianity is inwardness. Christianity is paradox, and paradox requires but one thing: the passion of faith."

The journey to faith in Christ requires risk, and change. It is as anxiety provoking as undertaking a major trip to an unknown destination. Abraham undertook such a trip and became a model for faith. Life is such a journey. We never know what the future has in store for us. Unexpected challenges cause us to have to respond with decisions and actions that we never anticipated having to make.

In March 2000 I received a call to accept the position of Pastor of Amelia Plantation Chapel on Amelia Island in Florida. I had been living for fourteen years in San Antonio, Texas, where I was the Rector of Christ Episcopal Church, a large congregation in the historic part of the city. Before receiving this call I had anticipated completing twenty years at Christ Church and then retiring back to north-east Florida where we had lived for ten years before moving to Texas. It is true that I had been praying about my future, and was open to alternative possibilities, but I did not expect my prayers to be answered so quickly and in such an unusual way. I guess I did not rightly know what to expect. God surprised me with an option I had not considered.

Amelia Plantation Chapel is an interdenominational congregation, of mainly retired people from all over the nation, who moved to Amelia Island to enjoy its climate, environment, stunning ocean-side beauty, recreational amenities, and proximity to the city of Jacksonville with all its resources. I had worked in Jacksonville, was familiar with the area, and had many friends there. It was just where we wanted to move back to when we retired. But this was a job!

Did I really want to down-size that much, from a busy, multi-staff church in the heart of a major, diverse metropolitan area, where I was established? In addition, I was about to leave on a three month sabbatical as a Visiting Fellow at St. John's College in the University of Durham. The timing seemed odd. Yet I was about to be 59 years old, and was aware that I needed to decide what I wanted to do for the next ten years of my professional life. Did I want to continue to do the same thing in the same place, or did I want to try something different? There were enormous risks involved. I would have to take a cut in compensation for the first 18 months. There was no guarantee that the congregation would grow under my leadership. I would be exchanging a sure thing for something quite uncertain.

I, of course, talked it over with trusted friends, and wrote down the pros and the cons of moving. But what helped me the most was an article I read at that time in a business magazine, *FAST COMPANY*. It was an interview by Polly Labarre with philosopher and management consultant Peter Koestenbaum. He styled himself as a philosopher who helped leaders in business to be successful human beings. This is what he said which resonated with me and enabled me to move forward in my life's journey.

"How do we make truly difficult choices? How do we act when the risks seem overwhelming? How can we muster the guts to burn our bridges and to create a condition of no return?" The real issues are: "What kind of life do I want to lead? What is my destiny? How much evil am I willing to tolerate?" He quoted Kierkegaard, "Anxiety rules the human condition... it can serve as a powerful, productive force in your life. Anxiety is the natural condition. Anxiety leads to action. Anxiety is the experience of growth itself. It is what we feel when we go from one stage to the next. Go where the pain is." Koestenbaum went on to say, "One of the gravest problems in life is self-limitation. We create defense mechanisms to protect us from the anxiety that comes from freedom. We refuse to fulfill our potential. We limit how we live so that we can limit the amount of anxiety that we experience. But no significant decision – personal or organizational – has ever been undertaken without being attended by an existential crisis, or without a commitment to wade through anxiety, uncertainty and guilt."

After mulling these words over, I spent two hours with a counselor who had been helping me to explore issues relating to my personal identity and future priorities. After several days of working through the details, I made the decision to go forward to the next stage of my life, and embraced the uncertainty of the future over the present.

If you want to have faith, then you must be willing to do what God is calling you to do. What is it that he is calling you to do? Listen, open yourself to his inner voice, and you will hear. But you must be willing to act, to risk, to venture, as did Abraham. The reward is worthwhile.

6

STAGES OF FAITH

Some people enter into a full-blown faith all at once when they experience a spiritual conversion or personal encounter with Christ. More people experience a slow growth of their faith over a lifetime. The apostle Paul noticed this in his comments about the Christians at Thessalonica: "We ought to give thanks to God for you.. and rightly so, because your faith is growing more and more."[1]

When something grows, it develops from one stage to another. Shakespeare portrayed man as developing through seven ages:

All the world's a stage,
And all the men and women merely players:
They have their exits and their entrances;
And one man in his time plays many parts,
His acts being seven ages. At first the infant,
Mewling and pewking in the nurses arms.
And then the whining schoolboy, with his satchel,
And shining morning face, creeping like a snail
Unwillingly to school. And then the lover,
Sighing like a furnace, with a woful ballad

Made to his mistress' eyebrow. Then a soldier,
Full of strange oaths, and bearded like the pard,
Jealous in honor, sudden and quick in quarrel,
Seeking the bubble reputation
Even in the cannon's mouth. And then the justice,
In fair round belly with good capon lin'd,
With eyes severe, and beard of formal cut,
Full of wise saws, and modern instances;
And so he plays his part. The sixth age shifts
Into the lean and slipper'd pantaloon,
With spectacles on nose and pouch on side,
His youthful hose well sav'd a world too wide
For his shrunk shank; and his big, manly voice,
Turning again towards childish treble, pipes
And whistles in his sound. Last scene of all,
That ends this strange eventful history,
Is second childishness, and mere oblivion,
Sans teeth, sans eyes, sans taste, sans everything.[2]

Men and women develop through different stages in life so that the same person may appear in different roles, and may re-invent himself for the purpose. Opinions may change over a lifetime as new knowledge is received and assimilated. Faith is no different. Faith looks different at each stage of its growth. When we physically or emotionally develop, we change over the years. Our faith changes also. Let us look at these stages of faith and see what they can tell us about the process of change that is involved.

There have been several studies of the development of faith. During a time of great stress and challenge I came across *The Critical Journey: Stages in the Life of Faith*, by Janet Hagberg and Robert Guelich. It is a description of the spiritual journey which addresses the struggle to find meaning and purpose, the crisis of values and identity at mid-life, the quest for self-actualization, and the healing of early religious experiences. The authors' goal is to help their reader to understand where he is in his search and where others are on theirs. The sections on the journey inward, and coming up against a wall in my relationship with God, spoke to me about the stage I found myself in at the time. It was an accurate diagnosis of my condition. I found it invaluable as a guide to moving on to the next stage of my faith.

In another book John Westerhoff suggests four stages.[3]

The first two stages he characterizes as *faith's infancy and childhood*. That is when we experience faith from those around us. We don't actually have to choose faith for ourselves because it is part of our environment as children. Paul talks about Timothy being raised in the faith of his grandmother, Lois, and his mother Eunice.[4] Or we may go through a conversion experience, a born again experience and be babies in the faith, needing to be spoon-fed for a while. "Like newborn infants, long for the pure spiritual milk, that by it you may grow up to salvation."[5]

When people came to faith in Christ in my church in London we would ask them to attend the Nursery Class, so named because it represented where they were in their faith. Like babies and young children it is a beautiful stage when people are open, innocent, sincere and delightful. We affiliate with the faith of our church, or youth group, or denomination. That is why young people can be so enthusiastic about their faith. They have accepted what they have been taught, and can be intolerant of those who disagree with them.

The third stage is *faith's adolescence* when we begin to question everything in order to decide what we are prepared to believe. It is part of individuation, of becoming our own person rather than being the clone of our community or peer group. Westerhoff calls this 'searching faith'. It is healthy to question so that we can make choices for ourselves that mean something to us. If this stage is discouraged, it can drive seekers into negative options. They may walk out of their rigid church, or their high-control family, in search of freedom of inquiry. Or, if they stay in their group, they may retreat inwardly and become angry and silent. Or, they may stifle their questions, and pretend to believe like everyone else, and sacrifice their integrity. Later in life searchers who have stifled their growth may blame their repressive churches, or their dogmatic parents, for their indifference. But we all have to take responsibility for our own growth in faith.

I can remember, when I was Dean of the Chapel at Gordon College, there was a student who would not attend chapel, or participate in an alternate chapel program of small discussion groups. He was in a high state of rebellion against his father, and all that he represented as a prominent Baptist pastor. In the end I met with him one on one and we discussed anything he wanted to talk about. He worked through his adolescent questioning, went through a failed marriage, and is now a successful Christian writer, and a practicing Roman Catholic.

This stage can be prolonged way beyond what is healthy. We may call it a case of arrested development. The searcher may "slip into a holding pattern, forever circling, never landing, and thus effectively avoiding responsibility."[6] Although he may no longer be an adolescent physically speaking, the adult searcher becomes an agnostic, taking refuge in the questions as a means of keeping commitment at arm's length. The apostle James has this person in mind when he wrote, "he who doubts is like a wave of the sea, blown and tossed by the wind. That man should not think that he will receive anything from the Lord, he is a double-minded man, unstable in all he does."[7]

"If we let reasonable doubts linger indefinitely, they can make us spiritual hypochondriacs – or perpetual adolescents."[8] Paul talks about those who are "always learning but never able to acknowledge the truth.".[9] There is a time when you have to 'fish or cut bait'. You can't sit on the fence forever. Those who will not move, who will not get off the fence, are making the decision to remain immature. They play mind games with themselves and take refuge in intellectual excuses for not being able to make a commitment either way.

The fourth stage is *faith's adulthood*. This is when we own our faith in Christ as authentically ours and not just borrowed from someone else, or something we profess in order to fit in with others. It has to do more with a personal relationship with Christ than the rituals of an institution.

Adult faith doesn't know all the answers, but is comfortable with trusting in God who does. The faith that has grown to this point is able to give up control to Christ and be comfortable in some settled convictions. The apostle Paul could say in the midst of his sufferings, "I know whom I have believed, and am convinced that he is able to guard what I have entrusted to him."[10] It is trust in the person of Christ, who, we are convinced, is able to deliver on the promises we have received, and our future well-being.

Where is your faith? What stage are you in? Are you beginning to wonder if your faith is simply a reflection of the group with which you have been affiliated all your life? Or do you feel unsettled, confused, doubting more than you are believing? Doubts need not be bad. Your questions may be genuine. They may need to be addressed in order for your faith to grow to the next stage.

On the other hand, how long have you been searching? If you find that you take more delight in withholding commitment, and you secretly resent having to close your options, be careful. Your well-fed doubt may really be a cop-out, and it may be time to move on. Don't be afraid to break out of your holding pattern and resume your flight plan! When we get stuck in our stage of faith, we are no longer growing. We can become hardened and defensive about where we are.

People get stuck for all sorts of reasons. When we get stuck for long enough we get trapped, and we may not know it. Our stage becomes a cage. "By this time you ought to be teachers... but you need milk like a child."[11]

Getting stuck occurs sometimes from our fear of facing the unknown. Other times it comes from crises that we cannot control. Or it maybe our fear that we cannot control God or our future. Some of us are never satisfied with our stage of faith. We are always looking for more information. We are insatiable learners in the faith. We go to every personal growth experience available. Self-growth can be addictive. We appear to be very open on the surface, true seekers of the truth. But we are closed just below the surface. We are simply afraid to surrender control to God. The risk is too high.

One of the difficulties in relating to others is that we become aware that they may be in a different stage from us. Being in a meeting with others at different stages from us can leave us perplexed and frustrated. It is like adolescents trying to understand what it means to be living in adulthood, or children trying to understand the inner life of seniors. For example, people at the adult stage, secure with what is right for them and with a strong sense of belonging, may think that those who appear to be questioning, or even rejecting their childhood faith, are not strong enough, not faithful enough, not willing enough, or just plain not Christian.[12] There have been times when I have been stuck in my faith development. I have lost my vision, or become disillusioned, or have felt depressed and tired. It is not that I have doubted God, but his presence has seemed less real than at other times. During one such period, I had to be prepared to listen to what God was saying to me rather than trying to keep in control of the agenda. I became aware that my shadow side consisted of those things I saw in other people that I did not like. I had to learn about forgiveness for myself and others. That led on to acceptance and love. Because of my vulnerability, I could sense God's presence in a new way. It meant asking why I was doing some things. It involved taking a risk in listening to what God was leading me to do that was different from before. I sang: "Spirit of the Living God, fall afresh on me. Melt me, mold me, fill me, use me. Spirit of the living God, fall afresh on me." All this required time away from my busyness, a time of solitude – time to reflect.[13]

Faith can go through all stages every day. Some of us find ourselves moving back and forth between stages of faith, searching awhile, and then reverting to childhood trust. There is nothing wrong with childhood faith. Jesus said that we must become children to enter into the kingdom of heaven.[14] Even mature faith keeps on searching, and sometimes cycling through periods of doubt.

Sometimes we cannot see beyond the present difficulties of life. In those times of darkness God gives us just enough faith to take the next step in the fog. We grow in faith as we trust that we are following Christ, even though we cannot see him clearly. Yet we believe that he is the Way, the Truth, and the Life, and that true Joy is to be found in going forward in faith, even when we do not completely understand.

King George VI, in his Christmas broadcast in 1939, when the United Kingdom was facing the Nazi threat, quoted Minnie Lou Haskins,

> "And I said to the man who stood at the gate of the year: 'Give me a light that I may tread safely into the unknown.' And he replied, 'Go out into the darkness and put your hand into the hand of God. That shall be to you better than light and safer than a known way.'"

Lord God, you know what stage of faith I am in at the moment. Enable me to move forward and not be stuck. Help me to let go of my ego, and to recognize that you are God, and to accept you as the Lord of my life. Enable me to be open to your direction. Direct my every thought, word, and action. May I experience your presence in my life, and respond accordingly. I surrender control of my life to you. May the love of Christ control me, and the power of your Spirit refresh me. Give me the courage to follow where you may lead, and to grow in faith, hope and love in my relationships with others. Amen.

7

QUESTIONING FAITH

For many years, my wife and I have sponsored a needy child through the work of *World Vision*. Four times a year their magazine comes in the mail. It is filled with stories of how children throughout the world are being helped by *World Vision*. But from time to time there are also heart-rending stories of the plight of millions more who need help. One issue predicts that by 2015, 40 million of the world's children will be orphaned by HIV/AIDS. Sub-Saharan Africa accounts for more than half of all HIV/AIDS cases worldwide. In 16 countries more than 10 percent of the adult population is infected. Poverty and ignorance increases the risks of infection and the mortality rate. Some people attribute evil to God, and claim that since he is supposed to be the author of all things that he should take the credit for HIV/AIDS, and other diseases. I have a local correspondent who sent me a poem by Philip Appleman to bolster his argument for atheism. It includes this stanza:

>I think that no one ever made
>a poem as powerful as AIDS,
>or plagues that may in summer kill

> half the bishops in Brazil
> and share the good Lord's Final Answer
> with clots and cholera and cancer –
> for God concocted pox to mock us,
> staph and syph and streptococcus:
> poems are made by bards or hacks,
> but only God makes cardiacs.[1]

Doubt rears its head in my life when I start entertaining difficult questions about the world. When I learn about primitive and poverty-stricken human beings, I ask myself how they can ever find life in all its fullness? I read about people with little hope, who live on the margins of life, like the huddled masses in Bangladesh, or the refugees in various countries of the world, and I ask what purpose God has for their lives? I see children who are crippled by land mines, or abused by parents, and I ask how God can be real and loving in the face of such evil? I see people who are mentally ill, or handicapped in other ways, and ask questions about how they can experience peace and joy in their apparent vacancy, watching television all day, doped up and chain smoking? I look at my own life and wonder how a person like myself, who has never unintentionally missed a meal, who has had the opportunity of education and travel, and never been unemployed, should be privileged and others deprived? I look up into the sky and realize that the universe goes on for billions of light years, and wonder how my life, or that of anyone on this planet can be significant? Are we just numbers, I wonder? How do we make sense of life?

What questions do you have? All of us have difficult questions that affect our ability to have faith, and give us reasons to doubt. Some of you might have questions about loved ones dying. When wars occur, and accidents happen, and tragedy strikes, we ask, "Why?" If there is a God in heaven how can these things happen? Where can we go with our questions?

I go to the book of Job. You know the story. Job loses his children, his livestock, and his health. He is destitute and depressingly sick. His friends come to comfort him but end up making him feel worse. Eliphaz accused Job of unacknowledged sin. Bildad said that he needed to repent and God would restore him. Zophar chimed in with similar advice. Their answers to the questions I raised would have been that it was God's will that other people suffer.

Job refused to accept his friends' shopworn belief that calamity had struck him because of his sin. I refuse to believe that people suffer and die because it is God's will, or because God wanted them in heaven, or that they are going to hell anyway. I want more of an answer than that. Just because I am a believer doesn't mean that I settle for simplistic explanations of life's problems. I struggle every day with the tragedies that I see on the television screen and in the newspapers. I have questions to which I have no answers as yet. I can identify with Job when he cried out to God, "Oh, that I had someone to hear me! ... let the Almighty answer me." (Job 31:35)

Job asked a lot of questions and he got his answers in the form of more questions which the Lord asked him (Job 38-41). "I will question you and you will answer me." (Job 38:3) In essence God said to him, "You cannot understand because you are not who I am. You have not existed as I have existed. You have not created as I have created. You cannot comprehend what I comprehend."

Gary Parker writes that he found three revolutionary truths in the book of Job that transformed his thinking about God's ways in the world.

"First, I discovered that God has no obligation to answer any of our questions. God came to Job and he comes to us not because we force him to answer, but because he chooses of his own free will to share his Person with us. When God spoke to Job out of the whirlwind, he did so not to give him all the answers, as if God were on trial, but to place Job on trial. We cannot hold God hostage to our questions." [2]

God has no responsibility to acknowledge, much less answer, all our questions. God's ways, as Isaiah puts it, are higher than our ways, and his thoughts are higher than our thoughts.[3] God graciously answers many of our questions, but he has no obligation to answer any. When we were children, we were asking "why" all the time. As parents we know we cannot answer them all to a child's satisfaction, and so we resort to having to say at times, "You'll understand when you grow up." Not every "why" of life has a reasonable answer. There are things we cannot understand, or as Job put it, "Surely I spoke of things I did not understand, things too wonderful for me to know."[4]

"Second, God does not count our questions as sin against us. Significantly, at the conclusion of the book of Job, God returns Job's wealth to him. Then God rebukes the three friends who had counseled Job incorrectly. God never changed his initial opinion of Job as "a blameless and upright man."[5]

The questions Job raises with God are legitimate. They are questions any human being in pain would ask. The Bible is full of examples of seekers after the truth that are asking good questions about the struggles of life.

There is no attempt in the Bible to silence discussion or debate. Christianity has always been at the forefront of enquiry, research and education. Our God delights in us using our minds to understand his creation, the nature of grace and the problem of evil.

"Third, the questions we ask can carry us into a deeper understanding of God than we have ever previously enjoyed. Job would never have known God on such an intimate level if he had not dared to express his pain and uncertainties.

In Genesis 32 we read how Jacob wrestled with God. In that encounter Jacob moved from a superficial relationship with the Lord into a face-to-face fellowship. At the conclusion of that dramatic episode Jacob said, "I have seen God face to face." In a similar fashion, Job admitted, "My ears had heard of you but now my eyes have seen you." (Job 42:5) When we wrestle with God honestly and openly, we have the grand opportunity to develop a deeper intimacy than does anyone who stands at a distance and waves a cheery hand."

"The honest struggle of Job with God can become helpful to us in our movement from doubt into faith… Through Job, and through other biblical stories, we see that God does not condemn us for our uncertainty. Instead, through the Job story we learn that God would much prefer our honest doubts to a dishonest faith. After all, God is the only one big enough to handle our uncertainties… Dr John Carlton once said, "God can stand our questionings much better than he can bear our indifference."[6]

When we find ourselves questioning the inequities of life, and we cry out in protest at the tragedies we see, God does not resent our questions, but welcomes them, for he cries out with us. It was God who heard the groaning of his people enslaved in Egypt and mounted a rescue operation using Moses. It was Jesus who reached out to the hungry, the poor, the crippled and the oppressed to heal them and give them hope. It was Jesus who wept over Jerusalem: "O Jerusalem, Jerusalem, you who kill the prophets and stone those sent to you, how often I have longed to gather your children together, as a hen gathers her chicks under her wings, but you were not willing!" (Luke 13:34)

The playlet *The Long Silence*, says it all.

"At the end of time, billions of people were scattered on a great plain before God's throne. Most shrank back from the brilliant light before them. But some groups near the front talked heatedly – not with cringing shame but with belligerence. 'Can God judge us? How can he know about suffering? snapped a pert young brunette. She ripped open a sleeve to reveal a tattooed number from a Nazi concentration camp. 'We endured terror... beatings... torture... death!'

In another group an Afro-American lowered his collar. 'What about this/' he demanded, showing an ugly rope burn. 'Lynched... for no crime but being black!' In another crowd, a pregnant schoolgirl with sullen eyes: 'Why should I suffer,' she murmured. 'It wasn't my fault.'

Far out on the plain there were hundreds of such groups. Each had a complaint against God for the evil and suffering he permitted in his world. How lucky God was to live in heaven where all was sweetness and light, where there was no weeping or fear, no hunger or hatred. What did God know of all that man had been forced to endure in this world? For God leads a pretty, sheltered life, they said.

So each of these groups sent forth their leader, chosen because he had suffered the most: a Jew, an Afro-American, a person from Hiroshima, a horribly deformed arthritic, a thalidomide child. In the center of the plain they consulted with each other. At last they were ready to present their case. It was rather clever.

Before God could be qualified to be their judge, he must endure what they had endured. Their decision was that God should be sentenced to live on earth – as a man!

'Let him be born a Jew. Let the legitimacy of his birth be doubted. Give him work so difficult that even his family will think him out of his mind when he tries to do it. Let him be betrayed by his closest friends. Let him face false charges, be tried by a prejudiced jury and convicted by a cowardly judge. Let him be tortured.

At the last let him see what it means to be terribly alone. Then let him die. Let him die so that there is no doubt that he died. Let there be a great host of witnesses to verify it.'

As each leader announced his portion of the sentence, loud murmurs of approval went up from the throng of the people assembled. And when the last had finished pronouncing sentence, there was a long silence. No one moved. For suddenly all knew that God had already served his sentence."[7]

God did not stay in his ivory tower and issue pronouncements about the world. He came in Christ to suffer and die with us. His followers walk in his steps, and walk the way of suffering, not knowing the answers to all the questions that they and others have asked down through the centuries. Anybody who has walked with Jesus has wrestled with pain and suffering, and the dread of insignificance. That is why we walk by faith and not by sight. We follow despite not having all the answers. Because God allows freedom in the universe there will be tragedies, and God does not directly cause them. In fact, he actually grieves with us when we suffer them. The answers will come as we experience the love of God in the Cross of Jesus. For the Creator is also the Savior.

8

CHOOSING FAITH

In answer to those who questioned his credentials, and the source of his teaching, Jesus claimed that it came from God who sent him. But how do we know that this is the truth? Jesus said, "If anyone chooses to do God's will, he will find out whether my teaching comes from God or whether I speak on my own."[1] Lynn Anderson claims that the "very first and most important step toward faith in Christ is to decide whether or not you really want to believe and honestly face the reasons why you choose what you choose."[2]

Faith, when you get down to it, depends upon whether you choose to do God's will (if God exists), whether or not you want to do God's will. It comes down to motivation. If God exists, are you willing to respond to God's call in Christ or not? This touches on the heart, or the will, not just the head, or the intellect. Anderson maintains that doubt is "more likely to be rooted in hidden, internal reasons of the will than in conscious, intellectual searching."[3] People may give all sorts of reasons why they are not believers in Christ, but more often than not, they have chosen not to believe.

What are some of these hidden, internal reasons of the will which block the motivation to believe?

There is the psychological defense. Doubters see belief in God as a psychological crutch. They view believers as emotionally insecure who have invented God because they couldn't cut it alone. But what if we are created by God to be emotionally insecure without a loving relationship with him? What if we are designed by God to believe in him, and his absence leaves a vacuum in our lives which generates this need? The psychological need is a genuine need. Miguel de Unamuno said, "To believe in God is, in the first instance, to wish there may be a God, to be unable to live without him.... if I do believe in God...it is principally because I want God to exist, and next because He reveals Himself to me through my heart, in the Gospel, through Christ, and through history. It is a matter of the heart." That is why the Bible says "And without faith it is impossible to please God, because anyone who comes to him must believe that he exists and that he rewards those who earnestly seek him."[4] God rewards us with his love when we are genuinely seeking him.

Then there are the emotional needs not to believe in God. Our pride makes it difficult for us to admit we need God. Our relationships may be preventing us from believing – we don't want our friends to think that we have gone religious. This is called in the Bible, 'love for the world'. It would be ridiculous to refuse to accept that which we know to be true because we have an emotional need to appear self-sufficient and strong in the sight of others. Our pride and our secular friends will not last forever. They will fail when we most need emotional support. "The world and its desires pass away, but the man who does the will of God lives forever."[5]

Another, and current, reason for doubt, is that of history. Many, as children, have suffered abuse from authority figures, either in their families, or in the church, which has served as an extended family. There are "large crowds of doubters who have been scarred through betrayal by professing believers – relatives, ministers, priests, elders, business partners, mates, mentors, or media evangelists. Anger, disillusionment, and mistrust over this kind of betrayal easily become transferred to God. And, again, the transfer sometimes occurs at hidden, subconscious levels that may surface in the disguise of doubt."[6]

Allied to this reason for doubt is the history of religions in the world. There has been so much violence and suffering perpetrated in the name of God. The institutional Church, which has enjoyed a position of privilege and power, has often used its position to do terrible things in the name of Christ. There are many people who called themselves Christians because it gave them power, but they did not behave as authentic followers of Christ. Jesus said that, "Not everyone who says to me, 'Lord, Lord,' will enter the kingdom of heaven, but only he who does the will of my Father who is in heaven. Many will say to me on that day, 'Lord, Lord, did we not prophesy in your name, and in your name drive out demons and perform many miracles?' Then I will tell them plainly, 'I never knew you. Away from me, you evildoers.'"[7]

We must make a distinction, as Jesus did, between institutional Christianity and the genuine Christian. We do not worship the Church, but Jesus Christ.

Through the centuries much has been done in the name of Christianity that does not reflect the teachings of Jesus. When evil has been done in the name of Christ, it is not the will of God, but the will of sinful men. The early Christians were effective missionaries because they took care of their neighbors, the poor, widows, and others who were in need. They protected children, especially baby girls who were often thrown away at birth.

People reject Christianity because of the Crusades, and the terrible things done in the Holy Land by the Crusaders. It was a misguided movement that encouraged people to slaughter others for the sake of political, material and spiritual rewards. This had nothing to do with the teachings of Jesus, but more with the ambitions of men. The Spanish Inquisition was another attempt to control what people believed by those whose positions gave them power over others. Lord Acton was right, "Power tends to corrupt and absolute power corrupts absolutely."

Most genuine Christians live under persecution, and suffer in the name of Christ rather than make others suffer. You can't blame Jesus and his followers for all the evil that has happened in his name. Some missionaries exploited natives they were trying to convert, but most missionaries were faithful to the gospel of Christ and saved the natives, where they worked, from cruel barbarities. They established schools and hospitals, and gave hope to those they served.

While Muslims reject Christianity because of the Crusades, many Jews reject Jesus because of the Holocaust. The Roman Catholic Church has apologized for any errors and failures of some Catholics for not aiding the Jews during the Nazi Holocaust. Cardinal John O'Connor of New York expressed abject sorrow for anti-Semitism in churches through the years. Martin

Luther contributed to the problem with his hatred of the Jews. Luther was a genuine Christian, but he was sadly and grievously mistaken in his views about the Jews. In that instance, he did not live up to the ideals of Jesus. In contrast to the passivity of so many Christians and church leaders in Germany under Hitler, there was the heroic example of Martin Niemoller and Dietrich Bonhoeffer of the Confessing Church movement, who were willing to suffer and die rather than acquiesce to the official government policy.

Bonhoeffer, who was executed by the Nazis for being implicated in the plot to assassinate Hitler wrote from prison, "If we are to look more closely, we see that any violent display of power, whether political or religious, produces an outburst of folly in a large part of mankind; indeed, this seems actually to be a psychological and sociological law; the power of some needs the folly of others. It is not that certain human capacities, intellectual capacities for instance, become stunted or destroyed, but rather that the upsurge of power makes such an overwhelming impression that men are deprived of their independent judgment, and – more or less unconsciously – give up trying to assess the new state of affairs for themselves. The fact that the fool is often stubborn must not mislead us into thinking that he is independent. One feels in fact, when talking to him, that one is dealing, not with the man himself, but with slogans, catchwords, and the like, which have taken hold of him. He is under a spell, he is blinded, his very nature is being misused and exploited. Having thus become a passive instrument, the fool will be capable of any evil and at the same time incapable of seeing that it is evil. Here lies the danger of a diabolical exploitation that can do irreparable damage to human beings."[8]

If history can be a reason to doubt belief in Jesus, it also provides many good reasons to believe in Jesus. Atheism has resulted in terrible violations in human rights. Lenin, Hitler, Stalin, Mao Tse-tung were all perpetrators of great violence. Christianity, on the other hand, has been deeply involved in helping the poor, the disadvantaged, and the disenfranchised. Christians built great educational and cultural institutions. The positives of Christianity overwhelm the negatives. Nevertheless, our failures should cause us to be humble in our attitude toward others. There are nameless men and women who have humbly and courageously upheld the Gospel through the centuries, who have served in obscurity, who have given their lives to help others, who have left the world a better place, and who have struggled to do the right thing despite incredible pressure to do otherwise. The civilizing ideas of liberty, conscience and truth can be traced to Christianity.

Lastly, a person may be reluctant to have faith because he or she simply doesn't want to do things God's way. Many people do not want to become Christians because they do not want to have to obey or follow the teaching of Jesus. They don't want to give up their freedom to do their own thing. They want to spend their money on themselves and their selfish pleasures rather than see it as loaned by God to do his will. Stewardship, sharing and giving are a tremendous threat to this kind of person. It is not so much a matter of doubt and faith as a matter of choosing to do one's own will rather than God's will. It is not so much an intellectual reason to doubt as a moral one. Helmut Thielicke put it this way:

"If a person learns to bring God into the picture and therefore begins to believe, then he ceases to be so passionately self-willed. Looking back, he discovers that it was this very autonomy, this centering his life on his own ego, that made him seek unbelief and made him fear that faith would threaten his self-will."[9]

We choose whether to believe in Christ or not. We choose whether to follow Christ's teachings or not. We choose based upon all sorts of motivations, all sorts of hidden, inner reasons of the will.

If we have a problem in believing we need to be brutally honest with ourselves. We need to take inventory of our inner selves. Could there be any reason – either conscious or buried in our subconscious – why we might not want to believe? Take out that reason and look at it honestly and see whether it constitutes a genuine barrier to believe or simply an excuse to avoid submitting our lives to God's will.

Remember that Jesus said, "if anyone chooses to do God's will, he will find out whether my teaching comes from God or whether I speak on my own." If you choose to risk doing God's will by living as though God exists and has a claim on your life, you will discover whether the teaching of Christ comes from God or not.

Even if you discover that you honestly don't want to believe, at least the uncovering of your real motive will enable you to deal with your decision more openly and honestly. Or it may propel you forward to overcome your reluctance, and cause you to be willing to risk believing after all. You need to choose every day what you believe.

Soren Kierkegaard writes: "In the end the archenemy of decision is cowardice. Cowardice is constantly at work trying to break off the good agreement of decision with eternity... Cowardice settles deep in our souls like idle mists on stagnant waters.

From it arise unhealthy vapors and deceiving phantoms. The thing that cowardice fears most is decision; for decision always scatters the mists, at least for a moment. Cowardice thus hides behind the thought it likes best of all: the crutch of time. Cowardice and time always find a reason for not hurrying, for saying, 'Not today, but tomorrow', whereas God in heaven and the eternal say: 'Do it today. Now is the day of salvation.' The eternal refrain of decision is: 'Today, today.' But cowardice holds back, hold us up. If only cowardice would appear in all its baseness, one would recognize it for what it is and fight it immediately.

Whereas decision reminds us of the end to come, cowardice turns us away from finality... A good decision is our will to do everything we can within our power. It means to serve God with all that we've got, be it little or much. Every person can do that. In the end, failure to decide prevents one from doing what is good... This much is certain: the greatest thing each person can do is to give himself to God utterly and unconditionally – weaknesses, fears, and all."[10]

What does one have to lose? And consider all that one can gain. Jim Elliot's famous remark about mortal life and eternity is still profound: "He is no fool who gives what he cannot keep to gain what he cannot lose." He was martyred at age 29 trying to bring the gospel of Christ to the Auca Indians in Ecuador. The witness of his commitment made a profound impact on me at age 16, and resulted in my offering myself for the ordained ministry. I was not alone. His example spurred many to similar endeavor. His life and death brought forth much fruit.

THE SUBJECTIVITY OF FAITH

Enlightenment thinkers in the eighteenth century understood the world through the lens of experimental science. Believing that all phenomena operated according to universal natural laws, they judged every intellectual proposition according to the test of reason. Their attitude was one of skepticism of anything seeming improbable or unreasonable, one of questioning supernatural religion and divine revelation. The Enlightenment embraced the idea of progress, trusting in the perfectibility of humanity, and the gradual elimination of superstition and prejudice. Radical Enlightenment philosophers in Europe rejected Christianity as improbable and superstitious, considering the miracles of the Bible as mere hoaxes. They embraced Deism, a religion of nature and reason. The Deists' god, like a watchmaker having wound his watch, stood aloof from his creation, allowing it to run on its own according to natural laws. This distanced God from the world of people.

The Enlightenment made the search for faith more difficult by depersonalizing the object of faith. Because of the concern to establish the objectivity of truth, there has been the concentration on the necessity of having to agree with the facts of faith. This reduced the exercise of faith to acceptance of doctrine about God rather than personal trust in the Savior. People became brainwashed by the prevailing intellectual requirements for objective criteria for belief. This is not to say that doctrinal statements are not useful and necessary expressions of what we believe. The revelation of God was not a statement of faith, but a person, yet we must be able to state who that person was. Christianity is not an undefined mysticism. Being able to state its truth in words is essential if we are to understand its nature and be able to communicate it to others.

Today, while there are still some secularists who would deny it, there is a philosophical consensus that the Enlightenment dogma that there are universally agreed principles of human rationality is no longer accepted. There is no universal human reason to which we can objectively appeal. There is no single set of objective criteria by which all beliefs can be tested. There is no objective, rational authority that has displaced God. There are many different ways of reasoning. Different people at different times and places have differing concepts of what is true and rational. The criterion for truth is determined by the nature of the subject matter. The natural sciences and mathematics have their own criteria to evaluate the truth of their research. They utilize objective means appropriate to their disciplines, but such means are not appropriate to other areas of reality. What works for the physical sciences, such as biology, chemistry and physics, does not work for philosophy and theology. To claim that the Enlightenment has eliminated the spiritual, the supernatural, or the religious, because we have evolved to the point where scientific knowledge has disproved their claims, is to fail to appreciate the differences between areas of knowledge of each subject matter.

Roger Poole in his ground-breaking critique of objectivity, *Toward Deep Subjectivity*, defined it in this way: "Objectivity is what is commonly received as valid, all the attitudes, presuppositions, unquestioned assumptions typical of any given society... Objectivity in any given society in fact gets defined as the political and social status quo.... Objectivity contends that 'facts' have to be accepted if there is to be objective discourse. It is considered subrational to question the status of facts. In mathematics, physics, biology, chemistry there are facts. It is therefore evident to objectivity that all human ratiocination which claims to be objective should adopt the impersonal stance of the scientist... Objectivity has ended up as being the equivalent of that truncated fragment of rationality which is generally called scientific. In the scientific objectivity, the thinker is excluded from the thought, and the personal involvement of the thinker in his work is denied and frustrated."[1]

One of the problems with scientific objectivity as a way of understanding life is that it eliminates much of our experience of life – our sense-impressions, our emotions, and all the realities that make up our everyday world. In their place science substitutes a knowledge of the mathematical properties of the world. Instead of a total, complete human world filled with meaning, we are given a formula. Perception and experience is replaced with data, with mathematical abstraction. The philosopher and rationalists of the scientific revolution proclaimed that we can only know what we can measure.

Donald M. Mackay, a research scientist specializing in the functioning of the brain at the University of Keele in England, wrote *The Clockwork*

Image: A Christian perspective on science, in which he debunked the fallacy underlying many scientific arguments against Christianity. He called it 'nothing buttery'. "Its current philosophical label is 'ontological reductionism'. Nothing-buttery is characterized by the notion that by reducing any phenomenon to its components you not only explain it, but *explain it away*. You can debunk love, or bravery, or sin for that matter, by finding the psychological or physiological mechanisms underlying the behavior in question."[2]

To illustrate his point he asks an electrician to tell us what is on the board of a neon sign. The electrician can give a careful description in electrical terms what makes the sign work without telling us the meaning of the sign. He can fail to mention the advertisement or message of the sign. The illustration demonstrates that scientific language can give us an accurate, technical, nothing but, explanation without giving us the whole story, the point or significance of the apparatus. A scientific description of the universe is limited to the components but doesn't tell the whole story of life.

The ultimate reality for anyone is themselves. It is the individual, through his or her perception, who judges and evaluates the worth and meaning of life. "What one takes to be true, evident, obvious is a function of perspective. We select and arrange our impressions in accordance with our deepest fears or ambitions or both. Very often we are concerned not to find out what is true, but what will best support the argument or cause to which we are known to adhere, or which will show us up to be the brighter or the better man."[3]

Everything selected for the purposes of the argument, everything useful for the argument, is filtered through assumptions of the individual. These assumptions are already in existence. By a process of selection and exclusion, a worldview which is helpful and advantageous will be filtered through the hopes and fears, the expectations and the experiences of the subjective existing individual. What finally gets through to our mind is a set of perspectives which have been modified in the transmission of impressions.

We each have a private perspective on our personal history, which is shaped by our interpretation of what happens to us over the years. Every day we filter through a certain set of perspectives, and these integrate and stick together. We get used to them, they mold us to receiving a certain kind of perspective tomorrow. What is true for us is true because the way we view our personal history has shaped us into the people we are. When we argue for a certain point of view, we argue from the center of our personal history.

What is true for us is true because of our already existing structure of belief. "It is to a person who already exists, complete in his hopes and fears, complete in his perspective on his history, that one addresses one's arguments. He possesses already a vision of the world, a vision peculiarly his, which he has built up over the years with care and concern. What he does not want to understand, he will not accord the status of an argument. What runs against his interests, is not a 'fact'. What is antipathetic to his own view, is not 'objective'. What he disapproves of, is immoral. What he does, is right. What he stands for, is not to be questioned."[4]

Each of us, therefore, has an existing structure of belief, a worldview, a set of presuppositions or assumptions, a set of categories we have developed through which we interpret the data of our daily experiences to give life meaning. We have a set of lenses through which we view our lives and the world.

Faith is the decision I make on the worldview I wish to make my own. Faith is my perspective on which realities, which truth, which vision, I wish to make my assumption. It is my subjective, personal commitment to the reality that is compelling to me. It is my understanding of the reality that confronts me.

Jesus came into the world to confront each individual with the necessity to make a decision about him. Some people found it difficult to believe in him because they were looking for objective 'facts' to scientifically verify his claims. Jesus said, "This is a wicked generation. It asks for a miraculous sign, but none will be given it except the sign of Jonah. For as Jonah was a sign to the Ninevites, so also will the Son of Man be to this generation. The Queen of the South will rise at the judgment with the men of this generation and condemn them; for she came from the ends of the earth to listen to Solomon's wisdom, and now one greater than Solomon is here. The men of Nineveh will stand up at the judgment with this generation and condemn it; for they repented at the preaching of Jonah, and no one greater than Jonah is here."[5]

The fact, or sign, that Jesus provided was himself. Just as Jonah, delivered from death by drowning through the whale, was the sign in his day, so is Jesus in his day. The message of Jonah evoked an immediate response in the Ninevites. The message of Jesus should evoke a greater response because of who he is. The assumptions of the people precluded them from seeing Jesus as the God-Man. They could only see him as 'nothing but' a Galilean preacher. They could not see the Message he embodied. This is still the case today for many. Later generations would also have the evidence of the resurrection. Just as the Ninevites were affected by the resurrected Jonah, so many would be affected by the appearance of the risen Jesus.

Even the queen of Sheba (Yemen) had been prepared to make a long trip to hear the wisdom of Solomon. Yet the people hearing Jesus had no journey to make. He was in their midst but they would not perceive in him the reality of God. Therefore they would be condemned for their blindness and refusal to believe what was in front of their eyes.

Jesus goes on to say, "No one lights the lamp and puts it in a place where it will be hidden, or under a bowl. Instead he puts it on its stand, so that those who come in may see the light. Your eye is the lamp of your body. When your eyes are good, your whole body also is full of light. But when they are bad, your body also is full of darkness. See to it, then, that the light within you is not darkness. Therefore, if your whole body is full of light, and no part of it dark, it will be completely lighted, as when the light of a lamp shines on you."[6]

I have a responsibility to receive the light that shines on my life and illuminates my understanding. If I have good eyes (i.e. believing eyes that are not veiled by reductionist or skeptical assumptions), the light will fill me. If I have bad eyes (i.e. sinful, unbelieving eyes that filter out the message that God is sending me in Jesus Christ), I will not receive the light he brings. "The man without the Spirit does not accept the things that come from the Spirit of God, for they are foolishness to him, and he cannot understand them because they are spiritually discerned."[7]

The Pharisees, who refused to believe that Jesus was the Messiah when he healed the blind man, were characterized by Jesus as having bad eyes. "For judgment I have come into this world, so that the blind will see and those who see will become blind." Some Pharisees who were with him heard him say this and asked, "What? Are we blind too?" Jesus said, "If you were blind, you would not be guilty of sin; but now that you claim you can see, your guilt remains."[8]

The source of light, or truth, is outside me. I perceive it and interpret it according to my assumptions. When by faith I receive the light of Jesus as the lamp of God's truth, I will be fully illuminated. Faith is my subjective reception of the objective light of Christ, that enables me to interpret my other assumptions. Christ throws light on my world.

10

FAITH HAS ITS REASONS

What causes people to follow Christ, or to believe in other religions? Is it on the basis of evidence we have come to believe as compelling? What causes us to continue to believe when there is contrary evidence? What would we have done if Jesus had come to us and invited us to follow him? How would we have responded to him or to any other spiritual leader who invited us to believe in him?

We see this happening at the beginning of the ministry of Jesus.[1] He found Philip and said to him, "Follow me." Philip decided to throw in his lot with Jesus. Why? We have a clue from his remarks to Nathanael. "We have found the one Moses wrote about in the Law, and about whom the prophets wrote – Jesus of Nazareth, the son of Joseph."

Apparently Philip and others were convinced, on the evidence they had gathered, that Jesus was the promised Messiah (the one prophesied in the Hebrew Scriptures), who had come (as John the Baptist said), to 'take away the sin of the world.'[2] John had been preparing the way for the Messiah to come by preaching the necessity of undergoing a baptism to signify repentance for sins. Jesus fulfilled his description and

John pointed to him as the Lamb of God, the one who has surpassed him, the one who might be revealed to Israel. John the Baptist testified that Jesus was the Son of God upon whom he had seen the Spirit come down and remain.

Philip was therefore accepting the testimony of one whose authority he respected: John the Baptist. He had also heard Jesus speak, and he may have seen him heal the sick. As a result of this personal exposure to Jesus, the testimony he received from John the Baptist was verified enough for him to agree to follow Jesus.

This was not good enough for Nathanael, who cynically responded to Philip's enthusiasm, "Nazareth! Can anything good come from there?" Or, as Eugene Peterson puts it, "You've got to be kidding."[3]

What is enough reason to believe, for one person, may not be enough for someone else. I used to think that faith simply equaled commitment on the evidence. I thought that if you just laid out the evidence for the identity of Christ, people would have to believe. In other words, I thought that people could be persuaded to believe only on the basis of rational argument. While argument and persuasion can be part of evangelism, it is not the reason most people come to believe.

The rational side of our minds is only one way we see reality. Reason is not the only way we get to truth. We can find reasons to interpret evidence one way or another. All evidence requires interpretation. Much evidence in matters of belief is circumstantial. Would we have found belief in Christ easier if we had been with Philip or Nathanael? I don't think so. There were many others who saw the same evidence in the person and ministry of Christ who did not follow him. The

reasoning process is morally and practically neutral, which can be used for good or ill. Daniel Taylor, in *The Myth of Certainty*, writes,
"There is no more spurious use of reason than to suggest that reason demonstrates that faith in God is irrational. It simply is not so, and anyone who argues such does not understand the nature of reason or faith. They are also wrong, however, who claim that reason and evidence prove the existence of God. God is not reducible to proof and only our weakness makes us wish it were so....In fact, reason recedes in importance in most of the truly critical areas of the human experience, largely because there are forces at work with which reason is not adequate to deal.... Reason is not usually the crucial component of one's love for another (over-analysis may actually weaken the love by turning the beloved into an object), or of one's response to a work of art (unless one has to explain – rationalize – the response), or of what one ultimately values in life. Neither should it be the primary tool by which one evaluates a relationship with God...reason is simply inadequate for the task."[4]

Why then do we believe what we believe? Our belief is the way we make sense of our existence. It meets our inner needs for love, security or fulfillment. Most people unconsciously accept the belief of those around them, without thinking about it. Others search for their understanding of life and for their personal fulfillment. They seek an explanation of life. We accept or reject evidence presented to us based upon our beliefs. Philip accepted the evidence presented to him by John the Baptist, his reading and interpretation of the Scriptures, and his personal experience of Jesus. Nathanael was not ready to do that. He was cautious about trusting the recommendations of others. He was not prepared to give his allegiance to someone he had not yet personally evaluated. Jesus' credentials were not impressive to Nathanael. Nazareth? You've got to be kidding! How could a guy from a back-water like Nazareth be qualified to deal with the knotty problems of the world like the existence of so much evil and suffering, and the competing claims of so many religions?

Whether we agree with the faith of others or not, we live in a world in which there are many different truth claims. What do we do with them? Pluralism is the world view that allows for many different interpretations of the evidence, except the interpretation that there is only one way. Taylor writes,
"The pluralist expects to find many different perspectives in the world and does so, thereby confirming his or her outlook. He or she is likely to feel offended, or even threatened, however, by the person who claims there is only a single correct explanation of reality or a single right answer to a social problem....Each is immune to the arguments of the other, finding in them only further confirmation of their own position. We fend off competing world views because by threatening our present understanding of reality, they threaten our essential security.... Flannery O'Connor realized this when she wrote, 'my communications... sound as if they came from a besieged defender of the faith. I know well enough that it is not a defense of the faith, which don't need it, but a defense of myself who does.' When people defend their world view, they are not defending reason or God, or an abstract system; they are defending their own fragile sense of security and self-respect. It is as instinctive as defending one's body from attack."[5]

How do you remain faithful to your own belief and yet respect the beliefs of others? We do believe in the freedom of religion, and the freedom of speech, in this country. Such a belief requires the tolerance of a marketplace of ideas even when we disagree. Taylor quotes Kierkegaard, who counseled the greatest sensitivity for those who seek to lead someone from error into truth:

"First and foremost, no impatience... A direct attack only strengthens a person in his illusion, and at the same time embitters him. There is nothing that requires such gentle handling as an illusion, if one wishes to dispel it. If anything prompts the prospective captive to set his will in opposition, all is lost. The indirect method, loving and serving the truth, arranges everything, and then shyly withdraws (for love is always shy), so as not to witness the admission which he makes to himself alone before God – that he has lived hitherto in an illusion." [6]

This is how Philip handles Nathanael. Philip invites him to "come and see" Jesus for himself. When he does, Jesus greets him with the words, "Here is a true Israelite, in whom there is nothing false." He acknowledged that Nathanael didn't have 'a false bone in his body'. (Peterson) Nathanael, said Jesus, was a man of integrity, a man who was open to the truth. Jesus showed respect for this seeker after truth.

Nathanael was taken aback. "How do you know me?" he asked. Jesus answered, "I saw you while you were still under the fig tree before Philip called you." This must have penetrated to the core of Nathanael's being because he responded with a declaration of faith. Something profound must have happened under the fig tree when he was in prayer or communion with God. Perhaps it was some crisis in his life, some deep desire for truth which he was seeking at the time. Whatever it was, it convinced Nathanael that this was no ordinary man, no charlatan, but someone who knew him in the essence of his being, and loved him. Jesus knew him – knew all about him, knew all about his dreams, and his hurts, his frustrations and his weaknesses, his secrets and his sins, yet he valued him, was interested in him, wanted to be associated with him, wanted him to be on his team, and this was supposed to be the revelation of who God was? His response was immediate, "Rabbi, you are the Son of God, you are the King of Israel." The cynic is transformed into the convinced follower. What before was an interesting introduction to another teacher turned into a close, personal friendship. A personal experience of communion with God in Christ made all the difference.

Faith has its reasons to believe. We all need some evidence to believe. If we have experienced a personal relationship with Jesus, like Nathanael, an 'Ahaa' encounter with God, it is possible to continue to believe even when other evidence seems to count against our belief. In fact Jesus warned us that, "false Christs and false prophets will appear and perform great signs and miracles to deceive even the elect."[7] There will be times when personal tragedies, and counter-claims by other spiritual leaders, will try our faith. Such times, when there is room to doubt, will challenge us to deepen our trust in the one whom, we believe, knows us best and loves us most. We do not abandon our faith in Jesus just because other evidence would give us reason to jump onto another bandwagon. Because of our personal relationship with God as revealed in Jesus, we prefer to trust in him, despite contrary evidence. C.S. Lewis put it this way: "To love involves trusting the beloved beyond the evidence, even against much evidence...You are no longer faced with an argument which demands your assent, but with a Person who demands your confidence." (*On Obstinacy in Belief*)

Nathanael said of Jesus, "How do you know me?" Jesus says to you and me, "I know you, I see you in your deepest need. I know your longings, your fears, your hopes, your pain, your struggles. I love you. Come, follow me, walk with me in this journey called life, and I will lead you in the way everlasting."

11

THE GIFT OF FAITH

I graduated from university with a double major in History and English. History is important to me. I value the history of my culture, and enjoy learning more about the events that have formed the world in which I live. The history of my family educates me about the influences that have made me who I am. In the study of history I became very aware of how 'facts' can be interpreted by different schools of thought. No matter what the orientation of the historian we still have to deal with the actuality of historic events. Historical research involves collecting the data and coming to some conclusion about them. It was natural for me to approach my understanding of the Christian faith in that way. The historical fact of the person and ministry of Jesus, with his impact on the world, became an important part of my faith. But over the years I have seen many different interpretations of the life and significance of Jesus. The Bible itself has been analyzed and criticized by generations of scholars with their own axes to grind. Any bookstore shelf on Christianity is stocked with multiple interpretations of the significance of Jesus. Writers, claiming to be objective scholars, who occupy prestigious university posts, are constantly publishing new views about Jesus and the Bible. Who to believe? How important is history to faith? What credence do we put in the latest magazine or newspaper article purporting to reveal new evidence for debunking the traditional view of Jesus as God come in the flesh?

I have just read a New York Times review by Natalie Angier, of Sam Harris's book, *The End of Faith*. The reviewer is described as a writer on the subjects of atheism and science for The Times, The American Scholar and elsewhere. "Sam Harris presents major religious systems like Judaism, Christianity and Islam as forms of socially sanctioned lunacy, their fundamental tenets irrational, archaic and, important when it comes to matters of humanity's long-term survival, mutually incompatible. A doctoral candidate in neuroscience at the University of California, Los Angeles, Harris writes what a sizable number of us think, but few are willing to say in contemporary America: 'We have names for people who have many beliefs for which there is no rational justification. When their beliefs are extremely common we call them 'religious'; otherwise, they are likely to be called 'mad,' 'psychotic' or 'delusional.' The danger of religious faith, he continues, 'is that it allows otherwise normal human beings to reap the fruit of madness and consider them *holy*.'"[1]

What do we say to such writers? Soren Kierkegaard in *Philosophical Fragments* addressed these issues in 1844. There is nothing new in these kinds of criticisms of Christianity. There are writers in every age who repeat the same arguments. The following is a summary of Kierkegaard's response to the rationalists of his day as expounded by Dr. Murray A. Rae[2], to whom I am indebted for this material.

From when I first became a Christian in 1955, and worked in college student ministry, it was considered necessary to be able to counter the arguments of rationalists like Bertrand Russell with logical reasons for faith. I became adept at being able to cite historical evidence for the truth of Christianity. I interpreted history as providing positive arguments for the truth of the Christian faith. But critics of Christianity also can find historical arguments for their own position. The fulfillment of the prophecies, the signs of the miracles of Jesus, the nature of the incarnation and resurrection, the growth of the Church, and the effect of Christianity on the history of the world cannot *prove* the truth of Christ because there is no way to verify the claims. These events may serve as illustrations of the truth of Christ, but they cannot conclusively demonstrate them to be true. Even those who witnessed the life of Jesus had a hard time of identifying him as the Messiah because of the hiddenness and lowliness of his life. Jesus was aware of this when he explained why he taught in parables: "You will ever be hearing but never understanding; you will be ever seeing but never perceiving."[3]

The historical testimony of the Scriptures serves as the occasion through which we are confronted with the need to believe, but it is not in itself a sufficient ground of faith. Without the condition, or means of faith, which is given by God, historical testimony remains indecisive. "Apostolic witness has always to wait upon the life-giving breath of the Spirit."[4]

Those who have criticized the accuracy of the New Testament maintain that there is no historical evidence that Jesus is divine. Even if they have proved to their satisfaction that Jesus, as we know him in the Christian faith, never existed, it does not follow that the authors of the New Testament did not exist, or that Christ did not exist. The witness of the apostles to the person of Jesus at a point in time is historical evidence to which we must give or withhold assent. We are required to give an assent to a fact of history. That event is the way God has revealed himself to us. Truth about God cannot be the product of our own deliberations because of our own limitations. The only way we can know the truth about God is that God reveals it to us.

When Simon Peter confessed that Jesus was the Christ, the Son of the living God, Jesus replied, "this was not revealed to you by man, but by my Father in heaven."[5] The apostle was not capable of knowing the truth of the identity of Jesus except by the revelation of God. His human reason was insufficient to comprehend the truth about Jesus.

Christianity is a call to follow Jesus in the discipleship of obedience. To follow him by imitating the pattern of his life requires a body of reliable historical knowledge of Christ. The only Jesus we know is to be revealed in the pages of the Gospels. Those who are skeptical of the trustworthiness of the Gospels are providing themselves with the means of avoiding the challenge of the claims of Jesus upon them.

Jesus tells the parable of the Pharisee and the tax-collector[6] to those who were confident of their own righteousness and looked down on everybody else. It is a parable of two types of human beings. One, the Pharisee, is full of his own accomplishments, and boasts of them. The other, the tax-collector, is too aware of his failings, his sinfulness, his inadequacies, to even look up to heaven. The Pharisee is reminiscent of the type who is full of his own intellectual abilities, and who, subsequently worships himself, whereas the tax-collector humbles himself and calls on the mercy of God as his only hope.

"In *Judge for Yourself!*.. Kierkegaard adduces the contrast set forth in 1 Peter between sobriety and drunkenness to suggest that it is the Christian who sees and understands the Truth while the wisdom of the world merely clouds and distorts. With consummate wit Kierkegaard has someone of 'secular mentality' drunkenly proclaim, 'I stick to facts. I am neither a fanatic nor a dreamer nor a fool; I believe nothing, nothing whatever, except what I can touch or feel; and I believe no one, not my own child, not my wife, not my best friend; I believe only what can be demonstrated – because I stick to facts.' The soliloquy continues becoming ever more repetitive and ridiculous until finally in a drunken stupor the speaker admits, 'The only thing, I suppose, that would momentarily disturb me would be if someone had the notion to say that I was drunk, intoxicated – I, the coldest and calmest and clearest common sense.'

"The drunk's principles, of course, are the maxims of rationalism: Believe nothing, stick to facts, trust no one, insist on demonstration... Is this not a kind of madness? Even if it could be done, and Kierkegaard thinks it impossible, would adherence to such principles not constitute an impoverished and ultimately inhuman existence? To whoever believes it possible, 'the apostle says, "Become sober!" – and says thereby: You are intoxicated; unhappy one, if you could see yourself, you would shudder, because you would see that you are like an intoxicated man when he – disgusting! – scarcely resembles a human being."[7]

The rationalist is drunk on his own ability to pass judgment on what God (if God exists) can do. His logic is impaired by his addiction. He thinks it is irrational to believe in Christ. But irrationality is the contravention of some principle of logic. It is not illogical to claim that something which is inaccessible to human enquiry may be revealed to us by God. The alternative to reason is divine revelation, which calls into question the authority human reason has claimed for itself. God reveals the error of those who trust absolutely in their own intellectual capacity.

Reason must give up its claim to being the ultimate authority. God gives understanding through faith, but on the condition that human understanding recognizes its own limitations. Reason wants to presuppose what God can and cannot do. That is why human reason is offended by the Gospels' confession that in the human figure of Jesus, the eternal God is present extending an invitation to love and follow him.

Christianity confesses that the truth about Christ is learned neither by speculation, nor through imagination, nor by historical investigation, but rather by virtue of the gift of faith. Receiving the gift of faith brings about a radical transformation, a new birth, a conversion. This involves letting go the authority of human reason – the abandonment of all preconceptions about God, and about humanity in relation to God. If we are to receive faith then we must admit the limitations of our own rational capacity. Reason needs to be redeemed. St. Paul talks about personal transformation by "the renewing of your mind."[8]. When that happens "you will be able to test and approve what God's will is – his good, pleasing and perfect will."

The truth about Christ is not capable of being learned by reason because humanity's reason is infected by sin. So Christ has to give us the means to understand it. That means is faith. There has to be a repentance and a conversion – a new birth such as Jesus mentioned to

Nicodemus.[9] God has to come into our lives, by his Spirit, and give us the means to understand the truth, not only about God, but about ourselves.[10]

The sinner is bound – he is not in possession of freedom to make any choices. We cannot freely decide to repent of our sins and then present ourselves before God to receive his grace. Our knowledge and our freedom to choose are contingent upon the divine gift of grace. However we are free to respond to the grace that has been done for us and disclosed to us in Jesus. By coming among us as a human, God in Christ has made it possible for us to respond to him, but he also allows the possibility of rejection, because he comes anonymously in humility. God does not force himself upon us.[11]

How does God extend his grace to us so that we can receive the gift of faith? St. Paul tells us, "How, then, can they call upon the one they have not believed in? And how can they believe in the one of whom they have not heard? And how can they hear without someone preaching to them? And how can they preach unless they are sent...Consequently, faith comes from hearing the message, and the message is heard through the word of Christ."[12]

Hearing the word of Christ is the gift of grace. God's action of revelation is the means by which recognition and repentance becomes possible. The choice now confronts us as to whether we will respond in faith. It is not intellectual assent that is required, but the response of living in the light of the truth that has been revealed.

"Learning the Truth cannot be reduced to a work of the intellect. It is not the preserve of reason, or of the imagination, or of memory. Instead it is a way of life in the company of Jesus whose identity as the Truth is confirmed by those who have known his blessing along the way."[13]

Faith is a mode of existence, and only those who take the plunge, who venture out over the seventy thousand fathoms of water, are in any position to learn the Truth. "Understanding Christianity is like learning to swim: it is only when entering the water, when setting out upon the life of faith, that one begins to understand."[14] You cannot evaluate Christian faith from the point of view of philosophical detachment. That is like trying to swim without getting into the water.

"Faith is a matter of personal response to and trust in the God-Man who confronts us with the challenge to follow him... The first disciples came to recognize Jesus and confess him as Lord only in the act of following him."[15] That is the only way we may come to understand the essential truth of the Christian faith.

12

WHY I BELIEVE IN JESUS CHRIST

It would take more than a chapter to give you the reasons why I believe in Jesus Christ and follow him as my Savior and Lord. Those reasons have been accumulating over a lifetime. Some of them have been discarded or changed as I have grown older. Others are newer as I have experienced more of life. But if I were to distill the reasons I believe in Jesus Christ into this short chapter I would want to include the following.

The first reason is the existence of life itself. As I observe and participate in life I am aware of its incredible variety and complexity. The size of the universe, and the minute calibrations that are essential to sustain life, convince me of the reality of God who has created life for a purpose. Life does not make sense to me without the initiation and sustaining power of the Creator. As St. Paul put it, "he himself gives all men life and breath and everything else.... For in him we live and move and have our being."[1] Through the miracle of creation God provides the genesis and environment that makes life possible. "For from him and through him and to him are all things. To him be the glory forever."[2] The origin of life, the sustainer of life, and the end or goal of life is God. Which God? "For us there is but one God, the Father, from whom all things came and for whom we live; and there is but one Lord, Jesus Christ, through whom all things came and through whom we live."[3]

An atheistic view of origins does not make sense to me. To view the universe as nothing more than a gigantic organism, or a complex mathematical formula, or a biological computer, flies in the face of the reality of human identity and relationship. A purely secular, merely scientific view results in reducing life to naturalistic phenomena. It is an inadequate interpretation of human behavior that does not account for meaning, purpose, significance and value. Love cannot be defined in purely secular terms. Community cannot be sustained from solely secular psycho-sociological, political and economic perspectives.

Life that has purpose and hope to it necessitates a Creator who is personally involved and lovingly concerned for his offspring. That is why God continually communicated with his people through prophets, and why he came himself to intervene on our behalf. The Creator revealed his purpose through his spoken Word, and also through his Living Word, Jesus Christ. "In the beginning was the Word, and the Word was with God and the Word was God. He was with God in the beginning. Through him all things were made; without him nothing was made that has been made. In him was life, and that life was the light of men.... The Word became flesh and made his dwelling among us. We have seen his glory, the glory of the One and Only, who came from the Father, full of grace and truth."[4]

I believe that Jesus Christ is the human face of the Creator. Why do I believe that? Because his life perfectly reveals God to me. He acts as the Creator by exercising his power over nature: stilling the storm, multiplying the loaves and fishes, raising the dead, healing the sick, and defeating death. He acts as God by exercising the power to forgive sins, to proclaim the good news of the kingdom of heaven, and to pass divine judgment. He shows us the significance of human life, and its eternal value, through his life, death and resurrection,

Without a belief in eternal life, human life would be, as Thomas Hobbes put it, "solitary, poor, nasty, brutish, and short." Life, with all its meaning and significance, makes no sense to me without life beyond the grave. When my grandmother died I was 12 years of age. I simply could not believe that a life that was so valuable could suddenly cease to matter. Ecclesiastes in the Bible states the obvious: "God has made everything beautiful in its time. He has also set eternity in the hearts of men; yet they cannot fathom what God has done from beginning to end."[5] Jesus came to reveal the nature of eternal life, to assure us of it as a gift, through union with himself. As we live with him we enjoy the reality of eternal life. He is "the resurrection and the life. He who believes in me will live, even though he dies."[6] I believe that this is true, because I believe that he is the origin and source of life, and that he has defeated human mortality through his own death and resurrection on our behalf.

The second reason I believe in Jesus Christ is because of sin and evil. I grew up in the aftermath of World War II and learned from survivors of the horrors of Japanese prisoner of war camps and German concentration camps. A book that made a great impression on me as a youth, which was in our bookcase at home, was *White Coolies* by Betty Jeffrey. Published in 1954 it told the story of a group of 65 Australian Nurses who were evacuated from Singapore just before it surrendered in 1942. Two days later, their ship, the *Vyner Brooke*, was bombed and sunk by the Japanese. Twenty-two of the survivors were cold-bloodedly murdered and the remainder taken prisoner. In spite of the constant danger of discovery and consequent brutal punishment, Sister Jeffrey kept this diary as a record of three and a half years' spirited resistance in the face of infamous maltreatment. A few year's ago it was made into a movie, called *Paradise Road*, starring Glenn Close.

Later I became aware of the brutality of communist rule. The evils of totalitarianism were enough evidence for me to see the failure of atheistic ideology, and the necessity of being accountable to a God of justice and love. My own life, and that of the world, witnessed to the need of a Savior. The words of St. Paul accurately described the human condition: "so that every mouth may be silenced and the whole world held accountable to God... for all have sinned and fall short of the glory of God."[7]

The evils in the world, man's inhumanity to man: corruption, crime, terrorism, exploitation, the way mentally sick people transfer their pain onto their spouses and their children, anger, greed, selfishness, the need to be in control, and so the list could go on, cries out for justice, and redemption. I am convicted of my own sinfulness. My conscience is held captive to the Word of God. I have to deal with my own guilt and failure, my anxiety and despair. The words of St. Paul ring true of my self-awareness: "I do not understand what I do. For what I want to do I do not do, but what I hate I do... I know that nothing good lives in me, that is in my sinful nature. For I have the desire to do what is good, but I cannot carry it out. For what I do is not the good I want to do; no, the evil I do not want to do – this I keep on doing."[8]

I believe in Jesus Christ because he came to set me free from the compulsion to sin, and the condemnation for sin. By his atoning sacrifice on the Cross he broke the power of sin over me. In exchange for my sinful guilt he gave me his pure righteousness, so granting me forgiveness and acceptance before God. In addition he gave me the gift of his Spirit to enable me to choose freely for good. The personal intervention of God in Christ on behalf of the human race includes the infilling presence of the power of his Spirit to accomplish his purposes in us and through us. I believe in Jesus Christ because he made possible the redemption of the worst of people, and the transformation of their character. He came to heal the sin-sick soul, to make whole the conflicted personality, to set free the obsessive-compulsive and to reconcile those who are alienated. Because God in Christ is love, he can help me to love others, something I could not do in my own strength. Instead of expecting me to measure up to his high standards he came down to my level and offered to live in and through me. "Behold, I stand at the door and knock. If any one hears my voice and opens the door I will come in to him and eat with him and he with me."[9]

In St. Paul's Cathedral in London there hangs a large painting by Holman Hunt called *The Light of the World*. It portrays Christ holding a lamp in a dark garden and knocking at a door that appears not to have been opened in a long time, for it is covered with weeds. It has no handle on the outside for him to open it. The door stands for the human heart. Christ, the light of the world, seeks admittance into our lives, so that he might banish the darkness of sin, and death. Only we can open that door by faith. He will not force his way in. He offers his grace – his unmerited, unearned gift of salvation. He asks for us to respond in faith, by receiving what he freely offers.

It is this transforming power of Christ and his Gospel that makes him the hope of the world. Political programs and parties come and go, but the Gospel of the kingdom of heaven is eternal. It is that Gospel which has motivated people to improve the living conditions of people, and care for them in their poverty, and sickness. It is Christ who lives in the needy of the world and who motivates his followers to do something about their condition. "For I was hungry and you gave me something to eat, I was thirsty and you gave me something to drink, I was a stranger and you invited me in, I needed clothes and you clothed me, I was sick and you looked after me, I was in prison and you came to visit me."[10]

I believe in Jesus Christ because he speaks to my needs and the needs of a divided and hostile world. It is only in him that there can be peace. "For he himself is our peace, who has made the two one and has destroyed the barrier, the dividing wall of hostility."[11] He is the peacemaker and he calls me to follow in his steps and be a peacemaker also. He offers to produce the fruit of His Spirit in my relationships with others: love, joy, peace, patience, kindness, goodness, faithfulness, gentleness and self-control. These virtues I cannot practice without abiding in him, living with him, following him, on a daily basis.

Lastly, I believe in Jesus Christ because, as God is spirit, he is always present. He promised that he would be with us always.[12] That means that God is with me as I trust in him and follow where he leads me. It means I can do everything through him who gives me strength.[13] This does not mean that life is always sunshine, and the way is always smooth. To walk with Jesus means walking the way of the Cross, as well as the way of the resurrection. It means sharing in his sufferings, becoming like him in his death before attaining to the resurrection from the dead.[14] It may mean being rejected and misunderstood as he was. It certainly means being a servant to others, humbling oneself, as he did. Heaven may be our goal and our prize, but there is much to do and to accomplish in this life. We are to "run with perseverance the race marked out for us by fixing our eyes on Jesus, the author and perfecter of our faith, who for the joy set before him endured the cross, scorning its shame, and sat down at the right hand of the throne of God."[15]

Why do I believe in Jesus Christ? Because he is my companion and guide, my brother and friend, my master and mentor, my Lord and my God. He soothes my sorrows and heals my wounds. I come to him, when I am weary and heavy-laden and find rest. I take his yoke upon me, and learn from him, for he is gentle and humble in heart and I find rest for my soul.[16] He opens my blind eyes, and loves me, and calls me to serve him. He never lets me down. He has blessed me beyond measure. He is the treasure that is worth finding.

PART TWO

THE TREASURES OF FAITH

Russell Conwell, founder of Temple University, Philadelphia, in his famous *Acres of Diamonds* lecture, told the story of Ali Hafed, who was a wealthy man and contented. One day he was visited by an ancient Buddhist priest who told him how diamonds were made. He said that a diamond is a congealed drop of sunlight, and that diamonds were the most valuable of all jewels. Ali Hafed asked the priest where he could find such diamonds. The priest told him to find a river that runs through white sands and that there he would find them. The now discontented Ali Hafed sold his farm, left his family with a neighbor and went off in search of diamonds. He wandered all over the world without any success. Finally he came to Spain and in despair, his money all spent, he threw himself into the sea and perished.

Meanwhile, one day, the man who purchased Ali Hafed's farm led his camel to drink from the water of the garden brook. He noticed a curious flash of light from the white sands of the stream, and pulled out a black stone having an eye of light reflecting all the hues of the rainbow. He took the pebble into his house and put it on the mantel and forgot all about it.

A few days later the same old priest came to visit again. As soon as he saw the flash of light on the mantel he rushed up to it and shouted: "Here is a diamond! Has Ali Hafed returned?" After finding out that Ali Hafed had not returned, the farmer took the priest out to the garden where he had found the gem. They stirred up the white sands with their fingers and discovered more beautiful and valuable gems. If Ali Hafed had looked in his own backyard he would have discovered acres of diamonds.

In contrast, Colonel Sutter began the California gold rush when he found gold on his ranch as he was constructing a mill. Conwell's point was that God has given us great opportunities for achieving wealth where we live. We don't have to go to the other end of the earth to find treasure. It is a matter of seizing the opportunity that is offered us by using our imagination and applying ourselves with industry.

So it is in the matter of faith. God has located the substance of the treasure of faith near to us. We do not have to go far away to look for it. The treasure is in our own backyard. Believing that the treasure exists is one thing, but recovering it is another. That is why there are two senses of the word *faith*. *Faith* is the subjective way by which we seek to respond to God. *The Faith* is also the objective content of what we believe. Faith is a *verb* that requires action. It is also a *noun* that describes what we are acting on. The treasure of faith is to be found in the truths affirmed in the creed. Just as we evaluate the treasure we seek so we evaluate the worth of the Faith through its components. The Apostles' Creed seeks to answer the three questions asked by every religion and philosophy of life: Where do you come from? Who are you? Where are you going? Let us look at the contents of this treasure chest and see what they are worth.

I BELIEVE – THE CHRISTIAN'S PLEDGE OF ALLEGIANCE

The Creeds began to be used in worship as a means of expressing the faith of the Church. The earliest creed seems to have been simply "Jesus is Lord."[1] When a person was baptized they declared that Jesus was their Lord. They declared their loyalty and commitment to Jesus, and trusted in his saving work of the Cross and the Resurrection. As time went on, it became necessary for Christians to explain what that meant. What did Christians believe about God, Jesus, the Holy Spirit, and the Gospel? By the fourth century, the Apostles' Creed, as we now know it, was being used in the western church. It was the creed candidates for baptism were expected to profess before they were accepted into membership of the Church. Alister McGrath suggests that today it serves three main purposes:[2]

First, it provides a "brief summary of the Christian faith." It does not contain all that we believe, and there are parts of it we may not understand, but it does provide a map and context for the faith of the Church.

Second, it allows us to "recognize and avoid inadequate" or unbalanced "versions of Christianity."

Some people may prefer to emphasize one part of Christianity rather than another. The Creed provides a "balanced and biblical approach, tried and tested by believers throughout the centuries." There are many deficient views of Christianity around. The Creed helps us to think through areas of faith that we might otherwise avoid.

Third, it reminds us that "to believe is to belong." To become a Christian is "to enter a community of faith, which stretches back to the Upper Room. By putting your faith in Jesus Christ, you have become a member of his body, the Church, which through the ages has used this creed to express its faith. It gives you a sense of history and perspective." You share the faith with countless others throughout the world who pledge their allegiance to Jesus as Lord.

We begin with the words *"I believe"*, or *credo* in Latin, from which our English word *creed* is derived. What does it mean to believe, and what do Christians believe?

In Acts 16:22-34 we have the story of the baptism of the Philippian jailer and his family. A great earthquake had occurred, the foundations of the prison were shaken, the doors flew open, and every prisoner's chains came loose. The jailer woke up, and when he saw what had happened, he drew his sword, and was about to kill himself, because he thought that the prisoners had escaped. The two apostles, Paul and Silas, saw what he was going to do and called upon him not to harm himself, by assuring him that everyone was still there. What then happens is simply extraordinary: the jailer is overcome with emotion, and begs them to tell him what he must do to experience the salvation of new life that he had heard them singing about in the jail before the earthquake.

This is how Peterson describes the scene: "They said, 'Put your entire trust in the Master Jesus. Then you'll live as you were meant to live – and everyone in your house included!' They then went on to spell out in detail the story of the Master – the entire family got in on this part. They never did get to bed that night. The jailer made them feel at home, dressed their wounds, and then – he couldn't wait till morning! – was baptized, he and everyone in his family. There in his home he had food set out for a festive meal. It was a night to remember. He and his entire family had put their trust in God; everyone in the house was in on the celebration."[3]

Peterson translates *"believe"* as "put your entire trust in". When John Gibson Paton (1824-1907), a Presbyterian missionary to the New Hebrides, began to translate the Gospel of John into the native language, he had a problem finding an equivalent word for 'believe'. The natives were cannibals. There was no trust between them. They had no word for it. He asked one of his helpers to describe what he was doing. He told him that he was writing at his table. He then asked him what he was doing when he sat in his chair and lifted his feet off the floor. The native told him that he was resting his whole weight on the chair. That was the expression he utilized to describe what John calls 'believe'. To believe is to put one's whole weight on who Jesus is and what he has done. It is a relationship of complete trust with the person of Jesus Christ. To believe is to have a deep, personal relationship with Jesus Christ. It is to respond to an invitation by Jesus to become his disciple, his follower.

But what does that mean? Faith has to have content. You will notice that Paul and Silas spent the whole night telling the jailer and his family what it meant to believe in Jesus as Lord. They went on to spell out in detail the story of the Master. They probably covered the essentials of the faith just as they might be summarized in the Creed. To be baptized meant more than having a vague knowledge about an unknown God. He was introduced to God as Father, Son and Holy Spirit, the Holy Trinity, the birth of Jesus, the significance of his life and teaching, his sufferings and death, his resurrection and ascension, his coming again in glory, the establishment of the Church, the forgiveness of sins, and the promise of eternal life. What a seminar it must have been. It was so exciting and new to them that they never did get to bed that night. A new world had opened up to them: a world in which they discovered a God who loved them and was searching for them, to invite them into his kingdom. This was not a God to be placated and humored, but a God who wanted to live with you, and within you, and through you to bless others. To believe meant to trust in someone who wanted to know and be known by you. The more you got to know him, the more you loved him. It was like a marriage between Christ and his Church, the bridegroom and the bride. It was like discovering a treasure trove of priceless gems.

To believe means to trust in Jesus as Lord, it means to know what that means – faith with content, not just a blind trust, but an informed trust. It also means to become committed to all that. Courtship leads to the wedding at which the vows are exchanged. To believe in Jesus as Lord leads to baptism. The jailer and all his family wanted to be baptized that very night, and they were. In baptism God commits himself to the candidate, and the candidate commits himself to God, as revealed in Jesus. It is a joyful and willing surrender to God. It is a throwing open of the doors of our lives and inviting God to enter as our Lord and Master, to live with us forever.

The jailer was filled with joy because he had come to believe in God – he and his whole family. They had acted upon their belief. To believe is an active verb not a passive one. It is to obey the call. It is an act of the will to put your whole weight upon what you have come to understand as God's truth in Jesus.

To believe is more than knowledge. It is obedience to what you know to be true. I may believe that there is a plane flying to Atlanta. I may check out flight times and even make a reservation and purchase a ticket. I may travel to the airport and see people get on the plane. I may believe that the pilot can fly the plane and that the equipment is trustworthy. But unless I put my whole weight upon that plane, by committing myself to entering it, and sitting down, and allowing it to fly me to Atlanta, it is of no use to me. To believe in Jesus is to act on that belief, it is to obey what it is saying to me. It is allowing God to take hold of me and allowing him to take me where he wants me to go.

Faith is deficient when a member of a Church may give intellectual assent to what the Creed represents, or is willing to be associated with those who believe, and yet holds back from wholehearted commitment. Their faith is passive. They do not act on their professed belief. They do not obey what it is saying to them. They avoid allowing God to take hold of them and allowing him to take them where he wants them to go. They don't get on the plane. As a result their lives suffer from inadequate faith. They do not have the joy of faith represented by this Philippian jailer. They have a general, vague belief, but it does not have any specifics. Many of the words of the Creed are meaningless to them. They are stuck on the ground, and they never go any farther in their relationship with God. They are happy to have the benefits of church membership, but they don't feel any excitement about it, and could take it or leave it. For them, it is not a matter of life or death. Belonging to the church is not that big a deal. The issue of faith is not that important to them.

The Rev. George Docherty preached a sermon in New York Avenue Presbyterian Church, Washington D.C. on Feb.7, 1954, in which he urged that the words, "under God" be added to the Pledge of Allegiance. At that time the United States was engaged in a bitter struggle with communism. He said that the pledge lacked, "the characteristic and definitive factor in the American way of life, the fundamental concept of the Founding Fathers that the country exists because of God and through God. Indeed, apart from the mention of the phrase, 'the United States of America', this could be a pledge of any republic. In fact, I could hear little Muscovites repeat a similar pledge to their hammer-and-sickle flag in Moscow with equal solemnity."

Sitting in the congregation that morning was President Dwight Eisenhower, who had been baptized in that church and was serious about his faith. When he left the church that morning the President told the preacher that he agreed with him entirely and set the machinery into motion to get the words "under God" inserted into the pledge of Allegiance. Congress passed the bill and Eisenhower signed it into law on Flag Day, June 14, 1954.

The rationale Docherty used was that the nation was facing a theological war, not just a conflict between two political philosophies, or two economic systems. He claimed that it was a fight for the freedom of the human personality. To quote, "It is Armageddon, a battle of the gods. It is the view of man as comes down to us from Judaeo-Christian civilization in mortal combat against modern, secularized, godless society."

Docherty helped to define and clarify the nature of the ideological struggle that the nation was going through. The Apostles' Creed is the Christian's Pledge of Allegiance. It helps to define and clarify the nature of the identity of the Church. It challenges each person who says it with the choice of what he or she is willing to believe, trust in, and commit his or her life to.

It is possible to discover anew the joy of belief experienced by the Philippian jailer and millions of others down through the ages. It involves making a commitment to Jesus as the Lord of your life. By exploring the faith of the Church your faith will be completed, balanced, and made adequate to the challenges of life. God may shake your foundations, blow open your prison doors, and loosen your chains.

14

GOD THE FATHER ALMIGHTY

Most people believe in God, or some kind of God. Our god is that to which we give the highest priority in our lives. We can make a god of anything that we worship, i.e. give worth or value to. People worship at the shrines of all kinds of gods. But what is the God we profess to believe in through the Apostles' Creed? God is described as "the Father Almighty."

For some people the image of God as Father is a problem. When people have experienced inadequate or abusive relationships with men, and their fathers in particular, they find the image difficult. Modern feminists reject patriarchal images to describe God. They would change "Father" to a neutral term like "Creator", or want to include "Mother" in the title. Let me try to respond to these concerns by sharing what Dr Klyne Snodgrass, professor of biblical literature at North Park Theological Seminary in Chicago has to say about them.[1]

First of all, the use of the title "Father" has nothing to do with maleness. God is not a man. We do not say "I believe in God the Male Almighty". Analogy is always limited. Gender does not provide an appropriate description of God. The title "Father" has to do with origin, love, security, and care. It is a relational, not a sexual term.

Secondly, we must remember that all language about God is metaphorical. There are matriarchal images for God in the Bible but they are rare, and when they do occur, are similes (using "like" or "as"), which seems to place them in a different category from the use of "Father" as a specific title. "Can a mother forget the baby at her breast and have no compassion on the child she has borne? Though she may forget, I will not forget you."[2] "As a mother comforts her child, so will I comfort you."[3]

Thirdly, while practice may be changing quickly, in English, masculine language has the potential to be generic, but feminine language is specifically feminine.

Fourthly, the use of *Abba* (Aramaic for father), and the frequent use of "Father" by Jesus and throughout the New Testament (and the church's history), makes the term too important to cast aside. The relational aspects of "Father," "Son," and "Holy Spirit," are too important to be replaced by "Creator," "Redeemer," and "Sustainer."

Fifthly, use of feminine language for God is particularly open to abuse because of associations with birthing and nature, as is evidenced in the ancient fertility cults, and in the modern new age movement.

The idea that Jesus, and the early church preferred the title "Father", because they were sexist, or simply reflecting their culture is not borne out by the historical facts. The fatherhood of God was not a major expression in Judaism compared to other names and titles for God. In the Greco-Roman culture the pantheon of gods included the mother goddess who was very popular, Hera or Juno. There was also Artemis or

Diana, the twin sister of Apollo, Athena or Minerva, patroness of art and war, Aphrodite or Venus, the goddess of love, and Demeter or Ceres, the goddess of the harvest. Baal was the great fertility god of the Canaanites who was linked with the goddess Ashtoreth, or Asherah . The uniqueness of the Hebrew religion was its monotheism in the surrounding sea of polytheism. Jesus revealed God to be primarily relational. It was a revolutionary description of God when the god was conceived to be distant and aloof from humanity. To call God Father, and not balance that with a female deity, was going *against* the prevailing culture.

At one point in his ministry Philip asks Jesus, "Lord, show us the Father."[4] Jesus answered, "Anyone who has seen me has seen the Father....Don't you believe that I am in the Father, and that the Father is in me?" He talked about his relationship with God as Father, and his disciples' relationship with the Father. Jesus claimed to be the earthly expression of God the Father.

Sigmund Freud maintained that belief in God as Father was the projection from our experience of earthly fatherhood, of our need to have an ideal father. Paul, on the other hand, maintains the opposite, that the fatherhood of man is derived from the divine fatherhood. "I kneel before the Father from whom his whole family in heaven and earth derives its name."[5] The Scripture says that God as Father is not a notion that we project on God from our culture and experience. Rather, our earthly fathers, and families, are a flawed reflection of God's fatherhood. We do not call God "Father" naturally, but only by grace. It is only through the work of the Holy Spirit that we can call God our Father. "The

Spirit himself testifies with our spirit that we are God's children."[6]

John Stott writes, "Paul is saying not only that the whole Christian family is named from the Father, but that the very notion of fatherhood is derived from the Fatherhood of God. In this case, the true relation between human fatherhood and the divine fatherhood is neither one of analogy ('God is a father like human fathers') nor one of projection (Freud's theory that we have invented God because we need a heavenly father figure) but one of derivation (God's fatherhood being the archetypal reality)."[7]

Jesus gave us the enduring description of God as Father in his parable of the Prodigal Son. Helmut Thielecke, in his exposition of this parable, called it the parable of *The Waiting Father*. "The ultimate theme of this story... is not the prodigal son, but the Father who finds us. The ultimate theme is not the faithlessness of men, but the faithfulness of God."[8] The father in the story lavishes his love on his grasping son. He gives him his inheritance before he deserves it, just as God gives us all the promise of life to use as we will without restriction. He waits patiently for him to return home. When the son arrives back, broken and defeated, repentant and humbled, the father welcomes him with open arms, and restores him to favor with a great celebration. That is the picture of God as father in the Scriptures. It is the picture of God as love almighty.

The fatherhood of God reminds us that our existence, physically speaking, is dependent upon him. He is Father by virtue of generation. Our life flows from him. Yet he is also our Father who raises us. It is one thing to be a biological father, but many biological fathers do not raise their children. They are no father to their children. Yet, the Father Jesus describes is the one who is always in relationship with us. He wants to be with us, alongside us, to help us become all that we are meant to be.

Some children are raised by fathers who adopted them. The biological father is nowhere around, but the adopted father becomes the real father of the child. Howard Edington, wrote a book entitled, *"The Forgotten Man of Christmas"* in which he spoke of Joseph, the non-biological father of Jesus. He calls Joseph the designated father. He writes, "The term 'designated father' is my own. I understand it to mean 'designated by God.' I, too, am a 'designated father.' Because our three children are adopted, I have long been sensitive to the fact that there are two ways in which you can be a father. You can be a father *of* someone, and you can be a father *to* someone. To be the father of someone is simply a biological function. It has no great significance in and of itself. However, to be a father to someone means to care for them, to love them, to teach them, to play with them, to provide for them, to be tolerant when intolerance would be easier, to be patient with them when impatience would be more natural. It is infinitely more difficult to be a father to someone than to be the father of someone."[9] God is our adopted, designated father, fulfilling all those characteristics.

The Fatherhood that Jesus referred to is not that of every creature, but of those who are his sons and daughters by adoption. "How great is the love the Father has lavished upon us, that we should be called children of God."[10] We are children of God by grace and not by birth. "To all who received Jesus, to those who believed in his name, he gave the right to become children of

God – children born not of natural descent, nor of human decision or a husband's will, but born of God."[11]

The analogy of God as Father reminds us that we are all feminine in relation to God. We are members of the Bride of Christ. We talk of Mother Earth and Mother Church. We relate to God as in an intimate relationship of love.

Jesus chose to reveal the nature of our relationship to God as our Father. As his disciples, we are called to remain faithful to his teaching rather than change it to suit our preferences, as congenial as that may be. While admitting the problem, we should try to resist allowing our negative experience of human fathers, or men in general, or male ecclesiastical or secular hierarchies, to influence our relationship with God. God our Father is the champion of women, and we are created male and female in his image. Women and men are equally precious in his sight. If we see the nature of God the Father revealed in Jesus, then every woman and mother is affirmed, and every man should respect every woman.

We profess to believe that God is Father *Almighty*. God, by definition, is all powerful, yet he restrains his power to allow the universe to function, and choices to be made. Evil exists because God does not fully exercise his power. Just as a father has to let his children make choices in order to mature and learn, God does not seek to control us. Human society is a web of choices in which we impact one another. God's power is exercised in and through the complex relationships in which we find ourselves. But just as a child seeks his or her father's help, so God gives us the opportunity to pray. It is through prayer that he chooses to exercise his power, as well as through the process of cause and effect in nature. Paul tells us to pray that we might be strengthened with the power of God's Spirit to know the extent of the love of Christ. For God the Father is able to do immeasurably more than all we ask and imagine, according to his power which is at work within us.[12]

Jesus reveals God as a generous father who wants to give all that he has to his children. "Which of you fathers, if your son asks for a fish, will give him a snake instead? Or if he asks for an egg, will give him a scorpion? If you then, though you are evil, know how to give good gifts to your children, how much more will your Father in heaven give the Holy Spirit to those who ask him."[13] When we profess belief in God as Father, we say we believe in the gift-giving God, the spirit of Christmas.

What is your conception of God? What is your relationship with God? Do you see that God wants to have a personal relationship with you, and loves you, as a father loves his children? What a wonderful God to believe in, to rest your whole weight on, to trust with your life!

15

THE MAKER OF HEAVEN AND EARTH

The Apostles' Creed affirms that God is the Maker of life. In so doing it merely echoes the fundamental teaching of Holy Scripture. "By faith we understand that the universe was formed at God's command, so that what is seen was not made out of what was visible."[1] Or as J.B.Phillips paraphrases it: "And it is after all only by faith that our minds accept as fact that the whole scheme of time and space was created by God's command – that the world which we can see has come into being through principles which are invisible."[2]

By contrast, Stephen Hawking, in *A Brief History of Time* writes, "But if the universe is really completely self-contained, having no boundary, or edge, it would have neither beginning nor end: it would simply be. What place, then, for a creator?"[3] John Polkinghorne, in *The Faith of a Physicist*, answers, "Every place – as the sustainer of the self-contained spacetime egg and as the ordainer of its quantum laws. God is not a God of the edges, with a vested interest in boundaries. Creation is not something he did fifteen billion years ago, but is something that he is doing now."[4]

In the Creed we say that we believe that God is the Creator, that the universe is his idea, and that it is good. The creation story of Genesis makes it very clear that when God created the universe he saw that it was very good.[5] The universe is the good gift of a loving God. This has all sorts of implications for our lives.

William Barclay[6] says that belief in creation raises three questions which affect our everyday lives:
1. Which kind of a world do we believe in?
2. Why did God make the world?
3. How did God create the world?

Let me take them in order.

The first question is: which kind of a world do we believe in? The Creeds were written to counter misunderstanding. There were two main theories about the relation of God to the world. One was pantheism, which held that in some sense everything is literally God. God *is* the world and everything that is in it. This was the view of the Stoics. They believed that every person, creature, down to the soil and stones, has the divine spark in them. This view is found in certain New Age and Buddhist thinking today. Its conclusion is that the universe is God, that the universe is eternal, without beginning or end, that there is no individuality, and no distinction between human and divine.

The second theory is its opposite. The Gnostics and Manichaeans believed in dualism, the two principles of light and darkness, spirit and matter. They viewed the material creation as evil and either rejected the physical side of life through ascetic behavior, or thought salvation was entirely a matter of the spirit, and that it did not matter what they did with their bodies, so they became promiscuous. This theory separated God from the universe, and denigrated the value of the physical creation. Christianity, on the other hand, affirms the material world. "For everything God created is good, and nothing is to be rejected if it is received with thanksgiving, because it is consecrated by the word of God and prayer."[7]

The Creed reminds us that God is both involved in the world and yet is above and beyond it. God is both immanent and transcendent, in and beyond the world, continually creating the world and directing life. The Christian believes that God is neither contained in the world nor divorced from the world.

The second question is: why did God make the world? What purpose does the universe fulfill? For some people there is neither rime nor reason to the universe. It is all random, where chance rules. This is the big question which faces us all: why the universe, why does life exist at all, what are we doing here, is there any sense to history? If there is no God, then there is presumably no eternal reason for life. But if we believe that God created this universe, and all the life in it, then presumably there is a reason. My professor of theology at Durham University, Charles Cranfield, put it like this:
"We believe that God, constrained by no need, necessity, or loneliness, being eternally rich, blessed, and perfect in himself, of his pure grace, his love, which knows no cause outside itself, decided in his freedom not to be for himself alone but to create human beings to be the witnesses, and the whole universe to be the theater, of his glory.....in which the drama of God's praise is to be enacted, and that all the manifold life of nonhuman animate nature has its function to fulfill as a magnificent chorus in the drama in which humanity as the chief actor has its own special rational part to play."[8]

Cranfield uses the analogy of the artist who is writing a play in which the whole universe has a part. Every day we wake up to play our part in this drama of creation and salvation. We are put into situations in which the storyline develops. We improvise within the limits prescribed for us. We do not see the limits, and do not realize that we are on stage. Unselfconsciously, we choose our roles and cooperate with, or resist God in his production. When the curtain comes down on our lives, we get to read the reviews written by the author and perfecter of our faith.

The creation is designed for God's glory, and the salvation of the people he loves. Everything that happens in life, is meant to move God's purpose towards completion. There is a reason, a purpose, a meaning for this world in which we live. The knowledge of this makes all the difference in how we make sense of our lives. If we know that God is working towards our salvation through what happens to us, we can take heart that it is worthwhile.

The third question is: how did God create the world? The Bible tells us that God created the world by the word of his power. He spoke the world into being. The Scripture is more concerned for the "who" not the "how" of creation. There should be no conflict between science and faith on this issue. It is when theologians make scientific statements, and scientists make faith statements, that we get into conflict. Both science and theology are forms of truth, but they speak to different sets of questions. It is when we get involved in questions of human origins that we can get into conflict.

Kenneth Miller, Professor of Biology at Brown University, writes, "True knowledge comes only from a combination of faith and reason... What science cannot do is assign either meaning or purpose to the world it explores.... I believe that much of the problem is the fault of those in the scientific community who routinely enlist the findings of evolutionary biology in support of their own philosophical pronouncements. Sometimes these take the form of stern, dispassionate pronouncements about the meaninglessness of life. Other times we are lectured that the contingency of our presence on this planet invalidates any sense of human purpose. And very often we are told that the raw reality of nature strips the authority from any human system of morality."[9]

The debate about the beginnings of life is colored by the conclusions people on both sides have reached independently of the evidence they cite. The age of the universe, and the process by which life was made, is an open question, which is not, I believe, addressed in the Bible. The seven "days" of creation may be thousands or millions of years as far as God is concerned.

The difficulty we have today is that an artificial separation has been made between science and faith so that the impression given is that science has reduced life to nothing but material components. Naturalistic science, taught in schools to avoid religious entanglement, contributes to the creation of a society in which life has no meaning and purpose, the physical is not seen to be sacred, and behavior is a matter of individual preference without any ethical base. This is why we are perceived by the Muslim world to be a promiscuous civilization, where every sexual urge is acceptable. Life is considered cheap, and many live like alley cats, by the survival of the fittest, the law of the jungle. Such behavior is certainly not "consecrated by the word of God and prayer."

How we view our creation determines how we live. If we believe that we are made by God for the purpose of living to his glory, in a drama that fashions our salvation, we will live very differently from those who believe that they are only biological mechanisms, the product of chance encounters.

The view that God is the maker of heaven and earth has consequences for our lives. The Bible teaches that we are stewards, not the owners of creation. We hold it in trust. We are responsible for how we treat the world, and all the people in it. The first role given Adam and Eve was to work in the garden and take care of it. That is still our task today. We are to take care of the world in which we live. We are to treat it and all who live in it reverently, and use its resources rightly in the service of others and to God's honor and glory.

"Realizing that God is the maker of heaven and earth is important in another respect. Many people feel frightened and lonely in the world. They are overwhelmed by the thought of the immensity of space. The stars in the night sky seem to emphasize the brevity and unimportance of human life. The stars are billions of miles away, and move farther away from us with each moment that passes. The light from them now reaching us may have begun its journey centuries ago, long before we were born.

The doctrine of creation allows us to feel at home in the world. It reminds us that we, like the rest of creation, were fashioned by God. We are here because God wants us to be here. We are not alone but in the very presence of the God who made and owns everything. We are in the presence of a friend who knows us and cares for us. Behind the apparently faceless universe lies a person. The stars in the night sky are then no longer symbols of despair but joy – the same God who made them also made me and cares for me! They are even reminders of God's promises – and their fulfillment. (Genesis 15:1-6)"[10]

We are not just children of the universe, but through creation, the offspring of God the Father, "in whom we live and move and have our being."[11] But even more, we can become children of God, "for if anyone is in Christ, he is a new creation, the old has gone, the new has come."[12]

16

JESUS CHRIST

The coming of Jesus of Nazareth changed the course of history. The temples of the Roman Empire were replaced by houses of worship of the Christian church. As Boston's famous preacher, Phillips Brooks (1835-1893) put it:
"I am far within the mark when I say that all the armies that ever marched, and all the navies that ever were built, and all the parliaments that ever sat, and all the kings that ever reigned, put together, have not affected the life of man upon this earth as powerfully as that one solitary life – the life of Christ."

When Phillips Brooks came to Boston in 1869 to pastor Trinity Church, Copley Square, he found that the New England Transcendentalists were asking the question, "What is truth, and what are the canons for determining its authority?" The answer uniformly given was that the authority was within the soul, and faith was the direct vision of the truth. No special unique authority was accorded to the books of Scripture or to the person of Jesus Christ. Christ was spoken of with respect and even reverence as a great teacher, but he was associated on the same level with Socrates, Plato and Mohammed. The Transcendentalists like Emerson and Theodore

Parker argued that the truths of Christianity were true apart from the personal authority or personality of Jesus. Phillips Brooks countered by saying that Christianity was not a system of doctrine but a personal force which is "the nature of Jesus, full of humanity, full of divinity, and powerful with a love for man which combines in itself every element that enters into love of the completest kind. The message entrusted to the Son of God when he came to be the Saviour of mankind was not only something which He knew and taught; it was something which He was. The idea and the person are so mingled that we cannot separate them. He is the truth." [1]

When we affirm our faith in the words of the Apostles' Creed we do not say that we merely believe in the truth of Christianity, or that we believe in the teaching of Jesus. We say that we believe in Jesus Christ, the person, and all that he stands for and accomplished. That has been the faith of the church from the very beginning. We see it in what happened outside the Temple when Peter said to the man crippled from birth: "Silver and gold I do not have, but what I have I give you. In the name of Jesus Christ of Nazareth, walk."[2] Peter did not begin to tell the man about the teaching of Jesus. He commanded him to get up and walk in the name of Jesus Christ of Nazareth.

When people gathered around the healed man, Peter began to reveal to them the significance of what had happened. He directed attention to Jesus, whom God had glorified. He called him the Holy and Righteous One, and the Author of Life. "By faith in the name of Jesus, this man whom you see and know was made strong. It is Jesus' name and the faith that comes through him that has given this complete healing to him, as you can all see."[3]

When Jesus was to be born the angel told Joseph to give him the name Jesus, because he would save his people from their sins.[4] Healing was the outward sign that he could and would forgive their sins, and relieve them from a life of guilt and judgment. The man crippled from birth, and forced to beg for a living, is representative of all of us, crippled by our sins, our weaknesses, our rebellious willfulness, our handicaps, our hurts, our inability to live in the fullness of life as God meant us. It is not silver or gold, science or religion, that is able to heal us. Government legislation, lectures on philosophy or morality, or sermons on doctrine, will not liberate us from what paralyzes us. It takes the name of Jesus to free us, and strengthen us to become fully human.

As Malcolm Muggeridge put it, "For it is precisely when every earthly hope has been explored and found wanting, when every possibility of help from earthly sources has been sought and is not forthcoming, when every recourse which this world offers, moral as well as material, has been explored to no effect, when in the shivering cold the last faggot has been thrown on the fire and in the gathering darkness every glimmer of light has finally flickered out, it's then that Christ's hand reaches out sure and firm. Then Christ's words bring their inexpressible comfort, then his light shines brightest, abolishing darkness forever."[5]

Peter told the crowd in Jerusalem that God fulfilled what he had foretold through the prophets: that he would send the Christ, even Jesus, and they must listen to everything he told them. Jesus is the carpenter from Nazareth, and he is also the Christ of

God, the Messiah, foretold in the Scriptures. The title, *Christ* or *Messiah*, simply means the anointed one. Just as the prophets, priests and kings in Israel were anointed with oil as they entered into their vocation, Jesus was anointed with the Holy Spirit from conception, and in his Baptism. He was anointed the *Prophet*, revealing the whole will of God for our salvation. Jesus was anointed the *High Priest*, and has given himself a sacrifice for sin, and has made an atonement for us, so that we might be no longer estranged from God's love, and exiled from our heavenly inheritance. He was anointed *King*, to defeat our enemies and to guide, protect and strengthen us.

Who Jesus was, what he did, and how he is alive and active in the world today to heal and to save, to raise people from being beggars to leaping and praising God, released from captivity to the past, singles him out from other men. Socrates taught for 40 years, Plato for 50, Aristotle for 40, and Jesus only 3; yet those 3 years infinitely transcend in influence the combined 130 years of these 3 of the greatest men of all antiquity.

Jesus painted no pictures; yet the paintings of Raphael, Michelangelo, and Leonardo de Vinci received their inspiration from him. Jesus wrote no poetry; but Dante, Milton, and scores of the world's greatest poets were inspired by him. Jesus composed no music; still Haydn, Handel, Beethoven, Schubert, and Bach reached their highest perfection of melody in the hymns, symphonies, and oratorios written in his praise. Every sphere of human greatness has been incomparably enriched by the humble carpenter of Nazareth. But his unique contribution is salvation – he came to save us from our sins. Jesus means "God saves." Philosophy could not accomplish that - nor art – nor literature – nor music. Belief in Jesus Christ is the faith that he can break the crippling power of sin and bestow the glorious freedom of the children of God. All that this means is expounded in the ensuing articles of the Apostles' Creed. It is a veritable treasure chest of good news, more precious than silver or gold. Paul talked about the "unsearchable riches of Christ."[6] This does not mean that we can never find them, but that we can never exhaust the riches that Jesus Christ brings. We can never spend all the riches of Christ for we can never come to the end of them. The Creed attempts to describe the dimensions of those riches.

Jesus Christ is alive today, and holds out his hand to us, to lift us up to walk with him in faith. We believe that the good news is the person of Jesus Christ, who comes to live in us and through us. He wants to anoint us with his Spirit, and make us little Christ's, that's what it means by Christian. We are called to believe in him as our Messiah, our Savior, our Prophet, Priest and King.

17

HIS ONLY SON

JAG is one of my favorite television programs. One of the perennial themes is the relationship between father and son: between Harm and his lost father, and Bud and his emotionally conflicted father. In one episode Bud stepped on a landmine in Afghanistan and had to have his lower leg amputated. While in recovery he faced the challenge of rehabilitation in Bethesda Naval Hospital. His father did not meet him on his return to this country because he could not face his son's disability. A month went by and still he hadn't been to see his injured son. Finally Mikey, his younger son, confronts his father and challenges him to be a man and be supportive of his son. Bud needed that support as he attempted to walk again with a prosthesis.

Who among us has not benefited from, or been handicapped by, our relationship with our parents? All too often we experience dysfunction, competition, weakness, and disappointment in our families. The sins of the fathers are often visited onto the next generation. This is the condition of sinful humanity which has wandered far from God's intention for us. We struggle to be good parents to our children. We look and long for good, healthy role models. We hope and pray that our children and grandchildren will be healthy parents in their turn.

All this is by way of analogy, for the relationship between the Father and the Son in the Holy Trinity far transcends any earthly relationship. The Nicene Creed tells us that Jesus Christ is "the only Son of God, eternally begotten of the Father, God from God, Light from Light, true God from true God, begotten, not made, of one Being with the Father."

What is the nature of the relationship between the Father and the Son? Jesus said, "I tell you the truth, the Son can do nothing by himself; he can do only what he sees his Father doing, because whatever the Father does the Son does."[1] Jesus Christ acts only with the Father. He does not act independently of the Father, he cannot act independently of the Father. It is like a father and son partnership. Just as a son, in the same business as his father, watches his father at work, anticipating every wish and move, and performing everything as the father would do, so that the son reflects the father's will. There is an uninterrupted communion between the two. The result of this is that what the Father does, the Son does also, not in imitation, but in virtue of having the same divine nature. There is a complete unity of action between the Father and the Son.

This is what William Barclay says about this claim. "The salient truth about Jesus is that in him we see God. If we wish to see how God feels to men, if we wish to see how God reacts to sin, if we wish to see how God regards the human situation, we must look at Jesus. The mind of Jesus is the mind of God; the words of Jesus are the words of God; the actions of Jesus are the actions of God."[2]

St. Augustine emphasized the inseparability of the Father and the Son using the analogy of a flame and the light it sheds. "The generating flame is coeval with the light which it generates: the generating flame does not precede in time the generated light; but from the moment the flame begins, from that moment the light begins. Show me the flame without the light, and I show you God the Father without the Son."

Jesus goes on to say, "For the Father loves the Son and shows him all he does."[3] There is a continuing habitual love between the Father and the Son. "The unity between Jesus and God is a unity of love. We speak of two minds having only a single thought and two hearts beating as one. In human terms that is a perfect description of the relationship between Jesus and God. There is such complete identity of mind and will and heart that Father and Son are one."[4]

Jesus is motivated not by selfish or merely human motivation. He acts only in accordance with what the Father shows him. This action is shown in giving life, raising the dead and judging the world.

"For just as the Father raises the dead and gives them life, even so the Son gives life to whom he is pleased to give it. Moreover, the Father judges no one, but has entrusted all judgment to the Son, that all may honor the Son just as they honor the Father. He who does not honor the Son does not honor the Father who sent him."[5]

Jesus is stressing the unity of the Father and the Son. What is done to one is done also to the other. The inherent dignity of the Son and his intimate relationship with the Father make the dishonoring of him a very serious matter indeed. Jesus told the parable of the wicked tenants who killed the son and heir of the property. The owner had sent his son to collect his rent saying, "They will respect my son." But they killed him. The owner brought those wretches to a wretched end.[6] So it is with those who dishonor the Son of God.

Jesus goes on to say, "I tell you the truth, a time is coming and has now come when the dead will hear the voice of the Son of God and those who hear will live. For as the Father has life in himself, so he has granted the Son to have life in himself. And he has given him authority to judge because he is the Son of Man."[7]

Human eternal destiny is determined by our attitude to the Son. Those who are spiritually dead hear his voice, and those who have heard it with appreciation, and take heed, live. "What he means is this – a man's judgment depends on his reaction to Jesus. If he finds in Jesus the one to be loved and followed, he is on the way to life. If he sees in Jesus an enemy, he has condemned himself. Jesus is the touchstone by which all people are tested; reaction to him is the test by which all people are divided."[8]

Jesus refers to himself here as Son of God and Son of Man. He sees himself as the unique voice of God, and the True Human of divine origin. He is the heavenly figure of Daniel 7:14, to whom is given, "dominion, and glory, and a kingdom, that all the peoples, nations, and languages should serve him; his dominion is an everlasting dominion, which shall not pass away, and his kingdom that which shall not be destroyed."

The people of his day realized the implications of what Jesus was saying: "he was even calling God his own Father [uniquely and only, not just as the Father of all], making himself equal with

God."[9] "For Jesus to speak like this was an act of the most extraordinary and unique courage. He must have known well that to make claims like this would sound the sheerest blasphemy to the orthodox religious leaders and was to court death. The man who listened to words like this had only two alternatives – he must either accept Jesus as the Son of God or hate him as a blasphemer."[10] (W. Barclay)

Jesus invites us to hear him and take the step of faith to believe that he is whom he claims to be. The Creed reminds us that Jesus was not just a God-inspired good man: nor was he a super-angel, first and finest of all creatures, called 'god' by courtesy because he is far above men, which is what Unitarians and Jehovah Witnesses say today.

God is one, and he reveals himself to us as Father, Son and Holy Spirit. Jesus Christ is the human face of God. God stands with us, before us, behind us, alongside us, upholding us with his love in Jesus Christ. He is the only Son of the Father. As the Father said at his Transfiguration, "This is my Son, listen to him."[11]

Whatever the history of our relationship to our earthly fathers, the relationship of God the Father and God the Son is available to us always. Nothing can separate us from the love of God that is in Christ Jesus our Lord. God will support us, be there for us, at all times. Jesus is not ashamed to call us brothers and sisters, for we are of the same family.[12]

The good news that Jesus came to bring includes the promise that we can have a divine Father and Brother. "For if God is for us, who can be against us. He who did not spare his own Son, but gave him up for us all – how will he not also, along with him, graciously give us all things?"[13] God the

Father, gives us his own Son, and this generosity guarantees that, with the Son, he gives us all things we need for our salvation. He gives us all the treasures of the kingdom of heaven. John Calvin comments: "This passage ought to remind us of what Christ brings to us, and to awaken us to contemplate his riches; for as he is a pledge of God's infinite love towards us, so he has not been sent to us void of blessings or empty, but filled with all celestial treasures, so that they who possess him may not want anything necessary for their perfect happiness."[14] This is treasure indeed!

18

OUR LORD

Christianity is counter-cultural. It goes against many things our democratic culture values. I grew up believing the Jack was as good as his master, and that anyone who tried to lord it over others was to be taken down a peg. Rebellion against overbearing authority is built into our society. Freedom is prized above most anything. Hierarchy and aristocracy is to be opposed in favor of the rights of the common man. There is no place for absolutist claims to power and influence. The revolutions of the 19th and 20th century did away with European monarchies. The royal families that survived have learned to adapt to the present democratic realities. No one has an inherent right to be obeyed by virtue of his origins. We have learned that power corrupts and absolute power corrupts absolutely. Too many rulers have abused their powers. We shake our heads in dismay at the stories of corporate executives acknowledging that they cooked the books in their companies because they were ordered to do so by their superiors, even when they protested. Such defense is an attempt to avoid responsibility for one's own actions. Taking responsibility for oneself is a virtue which makes us suspicious of hierarchical systems. Yet we recognize the need for a chain of command, especially in the military. How do we reconcile our need for individual responsibility and the claims of Christ to be Lord of all, to be followed and obeyed?

In the story of the Roman centurion in the gospel, the soldier sends friends to Jesus to say to him, "Lord, don't trouble yourself, for I do not deserve to have you come under my roof. That is why I did not even consider myself worthy to come to you. But say the word, and my servant will be healed. For I myself am a man under authority, with soldiers under me. "I tell this one, 'Go,' and he goes; and that one 'Come,' and he comes. I say to my servant, 'Do this,' and he does it."[1]

This soldier recognizes that Jesus is far superior to him. He exhibits a humility that reflects an estimate of himself as an unworthy sinner, who is seeking for help for a loved one. I do not think that this is a man who has self esteem problems. He could not have risen to the position of command if he were inadequate. He is a man who recognizes power when he sees it. He calls upon Jesus for help in an area that he is helpless – healing. He does not command Jesus. To the contrary, he believes that Jesus need only say the right word, and his authority over this sickness will be communicated to his servant without him having to be present. No wonder Jesus says of him, "I tell you, I have not found such great faith even in Israel."

Could it be that it takes a man who has an awareness of his own worth, and unworthiness, i.e. he has a correct estimate of himself as valuable, and at the same time acknowledges the limits of his ability, to accept the superior power of the Lord? In other words, to accept the power of a superior requires an awareness of their *right* to command us. The chain of command in the military, or in any other enterprise (business, family, or government) is legitimized when the superior is seen to have *earned* his rank. The power to command cannot merely be inherited, it has to be earned if it is to be acknowledged.

In the Bible, God is called LORD by virtue of his position as Creator and Savior. In the Old Testament the word, LORD appears in the text when the sacred name of God appears. The name of God was too holy to be used, so a cipher of four letters YHWH was used, which is translated in the King James Version as Jehovah, or today as Yahweh. In the New Testament this name is applied to Jesus. In Philippians 2:10,11 Paul is using a quotation from Isaiah 45:23 referring to God:

"At the name of Jesus every knee should bow, in heaven and on earth and under the earth, and every tongue confess that Jesus Christ is Lord, to the glory of God the Father."

Time and again in the New Testament the faith of the Christian disciples is expressed as "Jesus is Lord." In Romans 10:9,13 we read, "if you confess with your mouth, 'Jesus is Lord,' and believe in your heart that God raised him from the dead, you will be saved. .. for, 'Everyone who calls on the name of the Lord will be saved.'" The last is a quotation from Joel 2:32.

Why is Jesus called Lord? Because he is the eternal Word, God the Son, the second person of the holy Trinity, who has entered humanity as Jesus, and has earned that right as the first born of all creation. It is a recognition of his divinity as Creator – "Who being in very nature God". It is also a recognition of his training and experience as a man.

"He had equal status with God but did not think so much of himself that he had to cling to the advantages of that status no matter what. Not at all. When the time came, he set aside the privileges of deity and took the status of a slave, became *human*! Having become human, he stayed human. It was an incredibly humbling process. He didn't claim special privileges. Instead he lived a selfless, obedient life and then died a selfless, obedient death – and the worst kind of death at that: a crucifixion. Because of that obedience, God lifted him high and honored him far above anyone or anything, ever."[2]

Why should we acknowledge him as *our* Lord? Not merely because he has inherited it, but also because he has earned it. Jesus deserves our personal obedience and loyalty because "by him all things were created." We owe him our physical existence. But also because, he loved us enough to come down from glory to human boot camp, and experienced what it is like to be human through the things that he suffered. He experienced death for everyone, and then overpowered death to rise again to new life so that he could give us the victory over mortality and condemnation for sin. He saved us from spiritual and eternal destruction. We owe him everything. If we have the sense of the Roman centurion we would recognize his authority to command, his power to heal and save, and realize our own unworthiness.

How do we acknowledge Jesus as our Lord? Intellectually and morally, by taking his yoke upon us and learning from him.[3] He becomes our teacher, and we become his pupils, his disciples, and we subject ourselves to his instruction and training. We "take captive every thought to make it obedient to Christ."[4] Dietrich Bonhoeffer wrote, "Only the person who follows the command of Jesus without reserve, and submits unresistingly to his yoke, finds his burden easy, and under its gentle pressure receives the power to persevere in the right way. The command of Jesus is hard, unutterably hard, for those who try to resist it. But for those who willingly submit, the yoke is easy and the burden is light."[5]

Vocationally, acknowledging Jesus as our Lord means being willing to have the same attitude as Jesus – of being humble enough to be a servant. If we claim to follow Jesus, it is inconceivable that we should spend our lives in any other way than in service. Luke Timothy Johnson writes, "If Jesus is our Lord, then none of us is lord over another. If Jesus is our Lord, then we can all be slaves of Christ, and none need be slave to any other human. Being slaves of the lord of the universe means that we are free from any enslaving creature and free to inhabit all of God's own freedom.... It is by confessing him as one Lord that we thus have the freedom to engage and change the structures that do not reveal but obscure his lordship over us all."[6]

Acknowledging Jesus as our Lord, societally and politically, means being concerned that his values will prevail, that human rights and human dignity be accorded to all races and religions, that honor be given to women and children, and that justice be secured for the oppressed. Christians down through the ages have suffered and died confessing Jesus as their Lord in societies that have denied him. They could not affirm that Caesar was Lord, and so they were condemned to die in the Roman Coliseum, killed by wild beasts. Wherever there have been totalitarian regimes of the right or of the left, dictatorships and ideological tyrannies, Christians have had to oppose them in the name of Christ as the only Lord.

Acknowledging that Jesus is our Lord in a pluralistic world is to affirm that "God exalted him to the highest place and gave him the name that is above every name, that at the name of Jesus every knee should bow, in heaven and on earth and under the earth, and every tongue confess that Jesus Christ is Lord, to the glory of God the Father."[7]

John Stott comments, "We have no liberty to place any limitation on the repeated word 'every'. Therefore, if it is God's desire that everybody acknowledge Jesus, it must be our desire as well. Hindus speak of 'the Lord Krishna' and Buddhists 'of the Lord Buddha'. But we cannot accept these claims. Only Jesus is Lord. He has no rivals. Mission is neither an impertinent interference in other people's private lives, nor a dispensable option which may be rejected, but an unavoidable deduction from the universal lordship of Jesus Christ."[8]

St. Augustine asserted: "Jesus Christ will be Lord of all or he will not be Lord at all."

Yes, Christianity is counter-cultural. At some point we have to come to a place in our lives, like the Roman centurion, and acknowledge our unworthiness, our limits, and God's provision for our needs. It means being willing to acknowledge that we have no power to help ourselves. It means humbling ourselves to accept the authority of a superior, a higher power in our lives. That power, the Christian affirms, is Jesus. He has come that we might be healed of our sicknesses, saved from our sins, and liberated to enjoy true freedom in the kingdom of God. He has earned our trust, and our obedience.

CONCEIVED BY THE HOLY SPIRIT, BORN OF THE VIRGIN MARY

On Friday, December 13, 2002, the Fernandina Beach News-Leader published an article by Bob Awtrey entitled, *"What is the Truth of Jesus' birth?"* He raised questions about the accuracy of the birth narratives in the Gospels. He concluded his article with this challenge: "As Christmas comes upon us, our town's gentlemen of the cloth should sort out all the foregoing for us.... Was there really a virgin birth? To which Nativity account should we give creditability, Matthew's or Luke's? We look forward to the advice of the readership in this matter."

I called Bob and had a conversation with him about his article and told him that I had planned to preach about the Virgin Birth and would send him a copy of the sermon. This initiated a correspondence which continues. He is a confirmed sceptic and rationalist who does not believe in the existence of God. I told him that I could not answer all his questions in one sermon but I hoped that I could convey something of the importance of this aspect of our belief.

The Annunciation, when the angel Gabriel came to Mary, is celebrated in the Christian Church calendar on March 25. Nine months later, to the day, Christians celebrate the birth of Jesus. St. Luke, a medical doctor, presents the evidence in his Gospel through the words of the angel Gabriel: "The Holy Spirit will come upon you, and the power of the Most High will overshadow you. So the holy one to be born will be called the Son of God... For nothing is impossible with God."[1]

The union of the divine and human described here is different from parallels from the Greek and Roman myths. In none of them is there any question of a truly virginal conception. What we find in the Gospels is not the story of some kind of sacred marriage or a divine being descending to earth and, in the guise of a man, mating with a human woman, but rather the story of a miraculous conception without the aid of any man, divine or otherwise. St. Luke describes a divine act of creation, using similar language to Genesis 1:2, "and the Spirit of God was hovering over the waters." It is not like the birth of Perseus or Hercules. God, who is Love, surrounds and generates the God-Man in and through the virgin Mary. The story is without precedent either in Jewish or pagan literature. Rupert Brooke tried to describe what it might have been like in his poem *Mary and Gabriel*.

Young Mary, loitering once her garden way,
Felt a warm splendour grow in the April day,
As wine that blushes water through. And soon,
Out of the gold air of the afternoon,
One knelt before her: hair he had, or fire,
Bound back above his ears with golden wire,

Baring the eager marble of his face.
Not man or women's was the immortal grace
Rounding the limbs beneath that robe of white,
And lighting the proud eyes with changeless light,
Incurious. Calm as his wings, and fair,
That presence filled the garden.
                                She stood there,
Saying, "What would you, Sir?"
                                He told his word,
"Blessed art thou of women!" Half she heard,
Hands folded and face bowed, half long had known,
The message of that clear and holy tone,
That fluttered hot sweet sobs about her heart;
Such serene tidings moved such human smart.
Her breath came quick as little flakes of snow.
Her hands crept up her breast. She did but know
It was not hers. She felt a trembling stir
Within her body, a will too strong for her
That held and filled and mastered all. With eyes
Closed, and a thousand soft short broken sighs.
She gave submission; fearful, meek, and glad....

She wished to speak. Under her breasts she had
Such multitudinous burnings, to and fro,
And throbs not understood; she did not know
If they were hurt or joy for her; but only
That she was grown strange to herself, half lonely,
All wonderful, filled full of pains to come
And thoughts she dare not think, swift thoughts and dumb,
Human, and quaint, her own, yet very far,
Divine, dear, terrible, familiar...
Her heart was faint for telling; to relate
Her limbs' sweet treachery, her high strange estate,
Over and over, whispering, half revealing,

Weeping; and so find kindness to her healing.
'Twixt tears and laughter, panic hurrying her,
She raised her eyes to that fair messenger.
He knelt unmoved, immortal; with his eyes
Gazing beyond her, calm to the calm skies;
Radiant, untroubled in his wisdom, kind.
His sheaf of lilies stirred not in the wind.
How should she, pitiful with mortality,
Try the wide peace of that felicity
With ripples of her perplexed shaken heart,
And hints of human ecstasy, human smart,
And whispers of the lonely weight she bore,
And how her womb within was her no more
And at length hers?
                Being tired she bowed her head;
And said, "So be it!"
                The great wings were spread
Showering glory on the fields, and fire.
The whole air, singing, bore him up, and higher,
Unswerving, unreluctant. Soon he shone
A gold speck in the gold skies; then was gone.

The air was colder, and grey. She stood alone.

    These circumstances of the conception and birth of Jesus are important enough to be enshrined in the Apostles' Creed. Its significance is that Jesus was a unique person who was the product of both the divine and the human in a manner unlike any others before or since. Dr. Jim Packer puts it this way:
    "The Bible says that the Son of God entered and left this world by acts of supernatural power. His exit was by resurrection-plus-ascension, and his entry by virgin birth... The entry and exit miracles

carry the same message. First, they confirm that Jesus, though not less than man was more than man. His earthly life, though fully human, was also divine. He, the co-creator, was in this world – his own world – as a visitor; he came from God, and went to God.

Second, these two miracles indicate Jesus' freedom from sin. Virgin-born, he did not inherit the guilty twist called original sin: his manhood was untainted, and his acts, attitudes, motives, and desires were consequently faultless."[2]

Why is this important? Christians believe that we are saved only through the sacrificial atonement of Jesus Christ, who substitutes his innocent and righteous life for our guilt and sin. If he is just a man, like the rest of us, he shares our need for redemption – in other words, he can't redeem us. He is part of our problem, not the solution to it. So there must be some essential difference between Jesus and the rest of humanity if he is to be our redeemer, our Savior. But if Jesus is God, and God alone, and only appeared to be human, he has no point of contact with us. He cannot represent us. He must be truly human if his sacrifice is to be authentic.

The divine-human nature of Christ, as seen in the Virgin Birth, enables him to be the mediator we need to reconcile us to God. As mediator he represents us to God and God to us. The central idea of the Virgin Birth, that Jesus is both truly God and truly human, portrays him as the perfect mediator between God and humanity.

Luke, the doctor, says in his narrative, "With God, nothing is impossible." Mary asks, "How will this be, since I am a virgin?" God can do the seemingly impossible. When we affirm our faith in the Virgin Birth we are affirming our belief that with God nothing is impossible, that he has his plan of salvation, his way of coming into our midst and using us to fulfill his purposes.

Those who find it difficult to believe in God, find it impossible to believe in miracles. Charles Dickens' Scrooge had to experience a change of heart before he could enjoy Christmas. That also was a miracle. The world without such miracles would be a sad and heartless place. Christmas is a season that celebrates the supreme miracle of the Virgin Birth.

Advent and Christmas are seasons of hope; when God breaks into our world to create new possibilities. God did a great thing through Mary, who was a very ordinary girl. He wants to do great things through ordinary people. God is still looking for human vessels through whom he can further his purposes. The Holy Spirit continues to come upon ordinary people. Mary was not the first or the last to whom God spoke. Her response to the angel changed her life, and the life of the world, and serves as a model for all who seek to be Christians: "I am the Lord's servant. May it be to me as you have said." She deserves her place in the Creed.

20

HE SUFFERED UNDER PONTIUS PILATE

Pontius Pilate was the Procurator of Judaea, the collector of taxes and enforcer of Roman law. He had full control in the province, and was in charge of the army of occupation: 120 cavalry and 4 or 5 cohorts, 2,500 to 5,000 infantrymen which was stationed at Caesarea, with a detachment on garrison duty at Jerusalem in the fortress of Antonia. He had full powers of life and death, and could reverse capital sentences passed by the Sanhedrin, which had to be submitted to him for ratification. He appointed the high priests and controlled the Temple and its funds. Even pagan historians mention Pilate only in connection with his authorization of the death of Jesus.

Philo of Alexandria, a Hellenistic Jew writing at the time of Jesus, can find no good thing to say about Pilate. He describes him as 'by nature rigid and stubbornly harsh' and of 'spiteful disposition and an exceeding wrathful man', and speaks of 'the bribes, the acts of pride, the acts of violence, the outrages, the cases of spiteful treatment, the constant murders without trial, the ceaseless and most grievous brutality' of which the Jews might accuse him. The verdict of the New Testament is that he was a weak man, ready to serve expediency rather than principle, whose authorization of the judicial murder of the Savior was due less to a desire to please the Jewish authorities than to fear of imperial displeasure if Tiberius heard of further unrest in Judaea. This is made abundantly evident by his mockery of the Jews in the wording of the superscription, 'Jesus of Nazareth, the King of the Jews.'[1]

Mention of Pontius Pilate in the Creed reminds us that we are dealing with historical reality, events which actually happened to people who lived in a specific time and place. "The gospel is not some fairy tale that happened 'long, long, ago and far, far, away'. Jesus and Pontius Pilate lived at a definite place and at a definite time. The gospel is not just about ideas – it is about God acting and continuing to act in history."[2]

Because Jesus suffered under Pontius Pilate, and it is recorded as happening by historians, it is impossible for anyone to deny that these things took place. They happened publicly, under the gaze of the citizens of Jerusalem. All could see what was going on. Mel Gibson's movie, *The Passion of the Christ*, has highlighted the nature of the raw brutality of the suffering of Jesus under the regime of Pontius Pilate.

"Pilate represents the rejection of Jesus Christ by his world – a major theme of the New Testament. This disowning of Jesus is seen as representing the rejection of the Creator by his creation. Jesus was condemned as a political threat to the stability and peace of the so-called *pax Romana* created by the Roman empire in Judaea."[3]

The sufferings of Jesus were politically, judicially and religiously afflicted. His sufferings were not due to sickness, or other natural causes such as financial reverses, or employment problems. They were deliberate acts of persecution by the world, the flesh and the devil. God in Christ suffered at the hands of sinful men. Peter, accused the crowd in Jerusalem in his Pentecost sermon: "You, with the help of wicked men, put him to death by nailing him to the cross."[4] Later, he said, "You handed him over to be killed, and you disowned him before Pilate, though he had decided to let him go. You disowned the Holy and Righteous One and asked that a murderer be released to you. You killed the author of life."[5]

It is still happening today. The Body of Christ still suffers. Paul referred to the suffering of the Church as part of the sufferings of Christ. "I fill up in my flesh what is still lacking in regard to Christ's afflictions, for the sake of his body, which is the church."[6] Christ's sufferings overflow into the lives of his followers. Paul talks about knowing Christ through the fellowship of sharing in his sufferings.[7] This is how we must see the rising persecution of Christians throughout the world.

In India, radical Hindus wielding machetes, swords, knives, iron bars and sticks attacked Joseph W. Cooper, 67, and five other Christians as they walked along a rice paddy embankment on January 13. The assailants also attacked pastor Benson K. Sam, his wife, Annie, and their children, Joy, Jeff, and Judith. Attackers struck Sam in the head and beat his wife and one daughter until they were unconscious. Villagers finally came to their aid, and the assailants fled. Hindu activists accused Cooper of violating his tourist visa by preaching at a church meeting. Since 1995 the government has banned foreigners on tourist visas from speaking at religious events. Hindu militants sought to bring criminal charges. Joseph Cooper was ordered to leave the country.

The core problem may be the increasing number of Dalits (outcaste or low-caste peoples) who are becoming Christians. Cooper said that the attack on him was a signal meant to put the lower caste and outcaste peoples in their place.

On March 17, 2002, an Islamic militant walked into the Protestant International Church in Islamabad, Pakistan, a church mainly attended by foreign diplomats and their families, and threw grenades into the congregation, killing five (one from Fernandina Beach, my neighborhood), and injuring 45. An attack in August on Taxila Christian Hospital west of Islamabad killed five nurses as they left chapel services.

In Nigeria, 400 died, 1,200 were injured, and 30,000 people were displaced by riots between Muslims and Christians. In Kano state, Nigeria, which has adopted Islamic Sharia law, government officials last year asked Christian clergy to approve the demolition of half the existing churches. Twenty churches had already been demolished by August when the decree was made.

In the Sudan, Senator John Danforth found tremendous human suffering during his tour of the region as the special envoy of the President. The Jihad that the government of the Sudan has waged against the south, imposing Sharia law, has resulted in the death of over 2 million people. The regime systematically burned crops, killed livestock, used its U.N.-sanctioned veto power to ban relief and required conversion to Islam for food. The Greater Nile Oil Project of the ruling regime in Khartoum – the National Islamic Front – propelled the clearing of land around the new oil fields. That meant the killing, displacing and enslaving of the southern population, which the Institute on Religion and Democracy in Washington, D.C. called genocide. I have a college friend who, as Provost of All Saints Cathedral in Cairo, was attempting to minister to thousands of these Sudanese Christian refugees.

In Indonesia, there have been ethnic cleansing of Christian enclaves. Radical Islamic groups are trying to rid Indonesia of any Christian presence. Indonesia is the world's most populous Islamic nation. More than 85 percent of its 215 million people are Muslim. Half a million Christians have been displaced, more than 5,000 killed, and as many as 7,000 forcibly converted to Islam. There have been more than 500 attacks on Christian churches since 1996. The town of Poso in Central Sulawesi is a tragic example. It used to have a population of 40,000, mostly Christians. By the end of 2000 it had been reduced to an exclusively Muslim population of 5,000 with all its churches destroyed.

In Vietnam in the last few years there were brutal campaigns to force Christians to sign documents agreeing to give up their faith. Many fled into the forest or to Cambodia. Amnesty International reported that people who were linked to religious groups that were not part of the state-sanctioned churches were frequently harassed, arrested and imprisoned. Over the past several years Hmong Christians have been charged with practicing religion illegally and jailed for up to three years, and forced by local authorities to recant their faith. In January, 2002, the Central Committee of Vietnam's Communist Party announced that it would establish cells of Communist Party members within the approved religious organizations. Alarmed Protestant leaders said that pressure will increase on the majority of Protestants.[8]

What can Christians do about the sufferings of the Body of Christ? We can pray with an informed mind. We can get to know websites and sources. We can raise the subject with Congressional representatives. We can urge the media to cover it more fully.[9]

Why are people wicked enough to cause suffering to those who follow Jesus? Because, like Pontius Pilate, and the authorities in Jerusalem, they reject Jesus. "It is sinful human nature itself that led creation to crucify its creator. Sin bites so deeply into human nature that it comes close to destroying our ability to recognize God when he comes among us."[10]

The words of Isaiah are still true today about the Servant of God, and his servants: "He was despised and rejected by men, a man of sorrows, and familiar with suffering. Like one from whom men hide their faces he was despised, and we esteemed him not."[11]

While the world exists there will always be suffering; there will always be people willing to suffer for the name of Jesus, there will always be people who reject Jesus, and want to make his people suffer. There will always be Pontius Pilates in this world, government officials who will aid and abet wicked people by having Jesus flogged, humiliated, and allowing those under him to strike Jesus on the face.

But we are called to stand with Jesus. We are called to share the suffering of rejection if necessary. We are called to believe in a God who loves us so much that he would come down to our level, and be willing to suffer for us and with us in order to bring us salvation. The suffering of Jesus proves that God loves us, and shares the suffering of his people. There are some things, so important, that they are worth suffering for. To know what they are, and to act on that knowledge, is to exercise faith in Christ.

21

CRUCIFIED, DEAD, AND BURIED

Some years ago I was visiting the National Portrait Gallery in London, which was showing an exhibition of Michelangelo's drawings. There was one unfinished painting entitled *The Entombment*, which portrayed Joseph of Arimathea, Nicodemus, Mary the mother of Jesus, Mary Magdalene, and another Mary, the mother of James and Joses. It is a powerful rendition of a grieving family, friends and disciples taking down the mutilated body of their beloved Master. I also viewed a red chalk drawing on pale buff paper by Leonardo da Vinci, on the same subject, entitled *The Deposition*.

Probably no event, apart from the Nativity of Jesus, has inspired more artists than the Crucifixion and the Descent from the Cross. All of the four Gospels contain an account of it. It is at the heart of the Christian faith. The Gospel writers made it very clear that Jesus died and was buried. The apostles made the fact of his death a central part of their preaching. The Cross became the chief symbol of Christianity. Everywhere we turn in the New Testament there is an insistence on the cross, the death, and the burial of Jesus, as the central act of our salvation. He died to make atonement for our sins.

The letter to the Hebrews sees the death of Jesus as the perfect offering to "cleanse our consciences from acts that lead to death, so that we may serve the living God." He is the High Priest who is the mediator who "died as a ransom to set us free from sins committed." His blood shed enabled us to receive forgiveness. "Christ was sacrificed once to take away the sins of many people."[1] In Paul's letters: "God demonstrates his own love for us in this: while we were still sinners, Christ died for us."[2] "He died for all, that those who live should no longer live for themselves but for him who died for them and was raised again."[3] John writes, "This is how we know what love is: Jesus Christ laid down his life for us.... This is love: not that we loved God, but that he loved us and sent his Son as an atoning sacrifice for our sins."[4]

This was God in action, truly human, truly divine, taking upon himself the whole burden of human sin, the guilt, shame and grief, and the dreadful weight of his own judgment. God bore it all for us, and in our place, in order to pardon us righteously and lovingly, without in any way condoning our sin. It cost God to forgive us.

My seminary tutor, Charles Cranfield, put it this way. "It is of vital importance that we recognize that it was God himself, and none other, that bore the cost. To think of Jesus as a third party besides God and sinful humanity, an innocent third party punished for the sins of humankind, would be to attribute to God an act of fearful horror. God did not lay the burden of our iniquities on a third party, but on himself – on his very self – in that human nature that his own dear Son, who is eternally God, inseparably one with the Father and the Holy Spirit, had for our sakes assumed. We must never forget that it is only within the framework of a proper Trinitarian doctrine of God that the Cross can be rightly understood."[5]

So you can see that the identity of the person who died on the Cross, and was buried, is of supreme importance. It only has significance for us if the person who was crucified, died and was buried is, as the Creed states, "Jesus Christ, his only Son our Lord". It was God the Son who acted as Mediator because he was also truly human. He can bring humanity and God together in reconciliation, breaking down the sinful barriers between us, by his sacrifice on the Cross.

From the beginning of the Christian era there were some teachers, called Gnostics, who suggested that divinity entered Jesus at his baptism and left him before his crucifixion. Cerinthus believed that it was Simon of Cyrene who was crucified instead of Jesus. In the apocryphal Gospel of Peter the cry of Jesus on the cross is: "My power, my power why have you forsaken me?" It is the cry of the man Jesus forsaken by the divine Christ. In the Gnostic Acts of John, Jesus holds a conversation with John on the Mount of Olives at the very time of the crucifixion, telling John that the crowds think he is being crucified, but in reality he is not suffering at all.

The views of these teachers are called Docetic, from the Greek dokein, 'seem', or 'appear'. Their view was condemned as a heresy because they taught that Jesus Christ's body and sufferings were not real, but apparent. They were wrong. They had the wrong idea about God. They saw God as detached and isolated, rather than involved and caring love. They had the wrong idea about Jesus. They did not take his humanity seriously. The church fathers said that, what God did not assume, he could not save. If God did not experience what we experienced in the body, his sacrifice would not be complete.

This view about Jesus was adopted in the seventh century by Muhammad, and is taught in the Quran. This is what the Quran says about the cross of Jesus Christ. "And because of them saying we killed Messiah, Jesus, son of Mary, the messenger of Allah. But they killed him not, nor crucified him. But the resemblance of Jesus was put over another man. And they killed that man. And those who differ there, are full of doubts. They have no certain knowledge. They follow nothing but conjecture for surely they killed him not, Jesus, son of Mary."

Islam maintains that it is inappropriate that a major prophet of God should come to such an ignominious end as crucifixion. They do not want to portray a God who is so weak that he cannot protect his own son. Why would God allow his son to be so treated?

God's majesty and transcendence are so emphasized in the Quran that any real engagement on his part with human sin and suffering is rendered impossible. Salvation for the Muslim is by way of obedience – submission, through the five pillars of Islam: recitation of the confession of faith, prayer five times a day, fasting during Ramadan, giving to the poor, and the hajj – pilgrimage to Mecca. There is no place for God to come down into our world, to suffer and die as one of us, for our salvation.

Their view of God is very different from that revealed through Jesus Christ.

"The prevailing view [of Islam] is that at some point, undetermined, in the course of the final events of Christ's arrest, trial and sentence, a substitute person replaced Him while Jesus Himself was, in a phrase, raised or raptured in Heaven from whence, unscathed and uncrucified, He returned to His disciples in personal appearances in which He commissioned them to take His teachings out in to the world. The Gospel they were thus to preach was a moral law only and not the good tidings of a victorious, redemptive encounter with sin and death. Meanwhile, the substitute sufferer bore the whole brunt of the historical crucifixion, having been sentenced and condemned *as if he were the Christ*."[6]

The Muslim argues that the death of Jesus is unthinkable because it is unnecessary from God's point of view. He believes that God can forgive unilaterally without having to endure any suffering. But forgiveness, by its very nature, involves suffering. According to the Muslim way of thinking forgiveness depends entirely on our repentance and on God's mercy, which in turn depends on what happens on the Day of Judgment, when our good deeds are weighed in the balance against our bad deeds. This means that we cannot be sure, here and now, of God's forgiveness, or of our final acceptance by him. Allah's forgiveness has to be earned and is never bestowed as a free gift on the undeserving. That is why there is no jubilant musical celebration in Muslim worship. There is no Amazing Grace![7]

"If Jesus did not die, then he ceased to be identified with humanity at the point which we fear and dread most of all. And if Jesus did not die, he could not in any sense defeat and overcome death. If there was no death, there can have been no resurrection. Yet the writer of the letter to the Hebrews speaks in the clearest terms of Jesus destroying the power of death through his own death: 'Since the children have flesh and blood, he too shared in their humanity so that by his death, he might destroy him who holds the power of death – that is, the devil – and free those who all their lives were held in slavery by their fear of death.'"[8]

John Stott tells the story of an Iranian student who was raised to read the Quran. "When Christian friends brought him to church and encouraged him to read the Bible, he learnt that Jesus Christ had died so that he might be forgiven. He said, 'for me the offer was irresistible and heaven-sent.' He cried to God to have mercy on him through Jesus Christ. Almost immediately 'the burden of my past life was lifted. I felt as if a huge weight... had gone. With the relief and sense of lightness came incredible joy. At last it had happened and I was free of my past. I *knew* that God had forgiven me, and I felt clean. I wanted to shout, and tell everybody.' It was through the cross that the character of God came clearly into focus for him, and he found Islam's missing dimension, 'the intimate fatherhood of God and the deep assurance of sins forgiven.'"[9]

What must it have been like to have been present when Jesus was taken down from the cross? Put yourself in the place of Joseph of Arimathea, or Nicodemus, or John, or one of the Marys. In their grief would they have questioned where God was in all his suffering? Despair and bewilderment would have been their experience Yet the story did not end there. "The apparently pointless suffering of Jesus was revealed as the means through which God was working out our salvation. God was not absent from that scene; he was working to transform it from a scene of hopelessness and helplessness to one of joy and hope. God's love was demonstrated, not contradicted, by the death of his Son."[10]

In the cross, death and burial of Jesus, God is saying to us that he is with us, even when our hopes seem at an end. "I have been there, I know what it is like," he says. "Don't despair. Trust me. I love you, and will bring you through. All will be well."

22

HE DESCENDED TO HELL
HE DESCENDED TO THE DEAD

This affirmation in the Creed directs our attention to the period between the death of Jesus and his resurrection. What did he do, and where was he, in the days between noon on the first Good Friday, and his resurrection on Easter Sunday morning? It also addresses the subject of, what we call the Intermediate State, what happens between death and resurrection. There is much conjecture about this subject, and many various interpretations of the Scriptures cited, so that theologians, preachers and teachers find it wise to refrain from claiming more than is absolutely necessary about what is a great mystery. I will give you an idea of the possible interpretations so that you can draw your own conclusions.

To those churches who omit this article John Calvin admonishes: "If any persons have scruples about admitting this article into the Creed, it will soon be made plain how important it is to the sum of our redemption: if it is left out, much of the benefit of Christ's death will be lost."[1]

The statement, *"He descended into hell"*, made its first appearance in the Apostles' Creed in 570, but it was used in other creeds from 359. The use of the word "Hell" has changed its sense since the English form of the Creed was fixed. Originally 'hell' meant the place of the departed as such, corresponding to the Greek *Hades*, and the Hebrew *Sheol*. Modern forms of the Creed substitute "the dead". Since the seventeenth century "hell" has been used to signify only the state of final retribution for the godless, for which the New Testament name is *Gehenna*.

J.I.Packer writes, "*Descended* does not imply that the place of the dead is down into the ground, any more than *rose* implies that Jesus returned to surface level at the resurrection. The language of descent is used because Hades, being the place of the disembodied, is lower in worth and dignity than is life on earth, where body and soul are together and humanity is in that sense whole."[2]

This article in the Creed states that Jesus, at his death, went to be with those who had died. He experienced, not only death, but departure from his body, before he assumed a new body in the resurrection. This is called, in Christian theology, the Intermediate State. That part of us, called soul, or spirit, by the will of God, and his power upholds and preserves us from dissolution. This soul, exists after death, separated from the mortal body, is really and truly in some place, present there, and not elsewhere. Jesus seems to indicate this possibility in saying, "be afraid of the One who can destroy both soul and body in hell."[3] The English Divine, John Pearson says about this state:

"That separate existence after death, must not be conceived to sleep, or be bereft and stripped of all vital operations, but still to exercise the powers of understanding and of willing, and to be subject to the affections of joy and sorrow. Upon which is grounded the different estate and condition of the souls of men during that time of separation; some of them by the mercy of God being placed in peace and rest, in joy and happiness; others by the justice of the same God left to sorrow, pains, and misery.... It will appear to have been the general judgment of the Church, that the soul of Christ, contradistinguished from his body... after a true and proper separation from his flesh, was really and truly carried into those parts below, where the souls of men before departed were detained; and that by such a real translation of his soul, he was truly said to have descended into hell."[4]

The primary passage of Scripture on which this statement in the Creed is based is Psalm 16:10, which is quoted by Peter in his sermon at Pentecost: "You will not abandon me [my soul] to the grave [Sheol or Hades], nor will you let your Holy One see decay."[5] Peter applies this to Jesus as a prophecy: "seeing what was ahead, he spoke of the resurrection of the Christ, that he was not abandoned to the grave [Sheol or Hades], nor did his body see decay."[6]

If the soul of Christ were not left in Sheol or Hades at the resurrection, then his soul was there before his resurrection; therefore after his death and before his resurrection, the soul of Christ descended into the place of the departed.

If this is so, what did he do there? What was the purpose of his going there? Many theologians say that it merely means that he experienced everything that we experience. He totally identified with us in our death experience. Others point to 1 Peter 3:18-4:6. "He was put to death in the body but made alive by the Spirit, through whom also he went and preached to the spirits in prison who disobeyed long ago when God waited patiently in the days of Noah.... The gospel was preached even to those who are now dead, so that they might be judged."

In the early Church it came to be believed that this is what Jesus did during his time in the place of the departed. He preached the Gospel to those who had died. Does this give the departed a second chance to believe? Or is the Gospel only preached to the saints of the pre-Christian era, so that they might see the promises fulfilled in Christ? Or does this mean that those who had never heard of Christ in their day, get an opportunity to do so? These questions became issues of controversy, and the medieval church created elaborate scenarios that speculated beyond the truth of Scripture.

One popular belief was called *The Harrowing of Hell*. In the apocryphal *Gospel of Nicodemus*, Christ breaks down the doors of hell, binds and tramples upon the foul spirits, and, taking Adam by the hand, conducts the saints to Paradise. This text had an enormous influence on the art and literature of the Middle Ages.

The core of truth in these Medieval fantasies is that Jesus perfected the spirits of Old Testament believers, and those who had trusted in the Savior without knowing him by name (Hebrews 11:40; 12:23). He made Hades into Paradise for the penitent thief, and for all others who died trusting him during his earthly ministry, just as he does now for the faithful departed (see Philippians 1:21-23; 2 Corinthians 5:6-8). His preaching to the spirits in prison, was of his kingdom and judgment, proving his supreme authority over all spirits: angels or demons. His actions in the place of the departed brought about great changes. He disarmed the powers and authorities, triumphing over them. (Colossians 2:14) He descended to the lower, earthly regions so that he might ascend on high, leading captives in his train, and giving gifts to men. (Ephesians 4:8-10) The widespread belief of the early Church was that the Lord released the souls of the Old Testament saints, and carried them with him to heaven.

William Barclay comments: "Here in symbolic language and picture is the answer to the question that has always exercised the minds of thinking people: What happens to the millions upon millions of men who have never heard of Jesus Christ? What happens to the great and good figures of the past who in every age and generation and in every race and nation lived nobly, but never had the opportunity to receive the Christian gospel because they lived before Jesus came? This doctrine means symbolically that either in this life or in the life beyond death all men are offered the gospel of the truth and love of God."[7]

J.Paterson-Smyth celebrates this understanding of the descent to the dead. "This was one of the gladdest notes in the whole Gospel harmony of the early Church for five hundred years... It was a note of triumph. It told of the tender, thoughtful love of Christ for faithful souls who had never seen Him. It told of the universality of His Atonement. It told of victory, far beyond this life. It told that Christ, who came to seek and save men's souls on earth, had continued that work in the world of the dead while his body lay in the grave. That He passed into the unseen world as a saviour and conqueror. That His banner was unfurled there and His cross set up there in the world of the departed. That the souls of all the ancient world who had never known Him, and WHO WERE CAPABLE OF TURNING TO HIM (i.e., who in their earthly probation, in spite of all their ignorance and sin, had not irrevocably turned away from God and good), might turn to Him and live. That the spirits of the old-world saints and prophets had welcomed Him with rejoicing. That even men of much lower place had yet found mercy. That even such men as those who had perished in the flood in God's great judgment, BUT HAD NOT HARDENED THEMSELVES AGAINST HIS RIGHTEOUSNESS AND LOVE, were not shut out from hope. In the 'many mansions' was a place even for such as they. To the teachers of the early Church, I repeat, it was one of the triumphant notes in their gospel – the wideness of Christ's Atonement."[8]

This interpretation does not give any encouragement to those who put off following Christ in the present, or who fail to seek first God's kingdom and his righteousness in their lifetime. The Scriptures teach that there is no opportunity of repentance beyond the grave or second offer of salvation for those who reject Christ in this life (Hebrews 6:4-6).

James F. Kay of Princeton Seminary, writing on this article, quotes John Calvin's view that the descent into hell refers to the sufferings of Christ on the cross: "The point is that the Creed sets forth what Christ suffered in the sight of men, and then appositely speaks of that invisible and incomprehensible judgment which he underwent in the sight of God in order that we might know not only that Christ's body was given as the price of our redemption, but that he paid a greater and more excellent price in suffering in his soul the terrible torments of a condemned and forsaken man."[9] Kay goes on to comment: "Christ died in the place of sinners (Isa.53:4-6). As such, he suffered in body and soul the torments of damnation, of God's severity, wrath and judgment. 'No wonder, then, if he is said to have descended into hell, for he suffered the death that God in his wrath had inflicted on the wicked!' This is shown in the 'cry of dereliction' from the cross: 'My God, my God, why have you forsaken me?' (Ps.22:1; Matt.27:46). Calvin comments, 'And surely no more terrible abyss can be conceived than to feel yourself forsaken and estranged from God, and when you call upon him, not to be heard.' In other words, hell in the Creed is defined by the cross of Jesus Christ. Hell is godforsakenness. To enter into this state is what it means to descend into hell."[10]

Jesus took upon himself the judgment we merited, and endured for us, as our substitute, so that we could be forgiven. He identified with all "suffering humanity in the grips and clutches of hell. By descending into hell, God in the person of Jesus Christ places the worst the can befall human beings within the redeeming embrace of the cross."[11]

The great biblical scholar Brooke Foss Westcott made this comment on the descent of Christ into Hades.

"It carries light into the tomb. But more than this we dare not say confidently on a mystery where our thought fails and Scripture is silent. The stirring pictures which early Christian fancy drew of Christ's entry into the prison-house of death to proclaim his victory and lead away the ancient saints as partners in his triumph; or again to announce the Gospel to those who had not heard it, rest on too precarious a foundation to claim general acceptance. We are sure that the fruits of Christ's work are made available for every man: we are sure that he crowned every act of faith in patriarch or king or prophet or saint with perfect joy; but knowing how and when we know not, and, as far as appears, we have no faculty for knowing. Meanwhile we cling to the truth which our Creed teaches us. To the old world, to Jew and Gentile alike – and it is a fact too often forgotten – 'the Under World,' 'Sheol' the place of spirits, was a place of dreary gloom, of conscious and oppressive feebleness. Even this natural fear of the heart Christ has lightened. There is nothing in the fact of death, nothing in the consequences of death, which Christ has not endured for us: He was buried, He descended into Hades, the place of spirits."[12]

Jesus went into the regions of darkness so that our souls might never come into those torments that are there. By his descent he freed us from our fears. "By his death he destroyed him who holds the power of death – that is, the devil – and free those who all their lives were held in slavery by their fear of death."[13] That is treasure indeed.

23

HE ROSE FROM THE DEAD

The cycle of nature repeatedly demonstrates resurrection to renewed life. Darkness turns to dawn. The new day begins. The ebb tide of the ocean turns and flows into fullness. The cocoon breaks open and the butterfly emerges as a different creature from its former state. Tiny seeds produce plants, bushes and trees, which in their turn drop more life-giving seeds

The history of the world reminds us of the rise and fall of civilizations, and their replacement by new movements, new leaders, new attempts to discover and establish new forms of government and societies.

The literature of humanity explores people's propensity for destruction, and their search for hope and meaning. There is a search by authors for ultimate justice, healing and resolution despite tragedy, crime and despair.

The choice that faces us is between fatalism, and destiny. We are either victims of a cosmic hoax, "a mist that appears for a little while and then vanishes,"[1] or we are designed by God for an eternal purpose. We are either purely material, temporal beings, one among many animals, or we are created to be living spirit-bodies.

The Bible tells the story, not merely of an impersonal universe, but a creation which is going somewhere. There is a storyline, a meta-narrative, that makes sense of it all. It is a story of a creation that needs to be rescued from itself. It is a story of people who need to be liberated from their circumstances. It is a story of second chances, new beginnings, resurrection and renewal.

It is the story of Abraham, the father of us all, who believed that God would give him back Isaac, even if he were killed and died. God would continue his line so that the promise would be fulfilled that his descendants would be as numerous as the sand on the seashore and the stars in the sky.

It is the story of Job, who lost all that he had except his life and his wife. He lost all his possessions, his children and his health. He longed for death. Yet God restored him and gave him a new life in rich abundance.

It is the story of the Israelites who are enslaved in Egypt, being liberated and given the Promised Land.

It is the story of the nation of Judea being conquered by the Babylonians and taken away as prisoners into exile for seventy years. There, between the Tigris and Euphrates rivers Ezekiel saw a vision of a valley of dry bones. As he looked the Lord breathed on them, they became whole, and came to life. "Then the LORD said to me:' Son of man, these bones are the whole house of Israel. They say 'Our bones are dried up and our hope is gone; we are cut off.' Therefore prophesy and say to them: 'this is what the Sovereign Lord says: O my people, I am going to open your graves and bring you up from them; I will bring you back to the land of Israel. Then you, my people, will know that I am the LORD, when I open your graves and bring you up from them.'"[2] This prophecy was fulfilled when they returned from exile to build a new nation.

Of course that is a selective reading of Biblical history. How we interpret history, our own, our nation's, or the events of the Bible determine how we see reality. Each of us decides for oneself what interpretation of life is ours. It is our belief system. It governs our understanding of life, and gives us the resources we need to manage the challenges of our lives.

When death, disease, and disappointment, enters our world, we have to meet it with an interpretive lens. When a loved one is afflicted, or we face loss of control, or we need answers to life's questions, we have to resort to some philosophy or religion. How do we know what is true, what will work for us?

Paul the apostle changed his mind on what he believed. He had persecuted the followers of Jesus, and supervised the stoning to death of Stephen, the first Christian martyr. But he had experienced an encounter with the resurrected and ascended Christ when he was on his way to Damascus to continue his persecution. His whole world had been turned upside down. The former zealot for bigotry had been transformed into a loving and caring missionary for Jesus.

He wrote to the Corinthians and reminded them of the word he had announced to them: that

"Christ died for our sins according to the Scriptures, that he was buried, that he was raised on the third day according to the Scriptures, and that he appeared to Peter, and then to the Twelve. After that, he appeared to more than five hundred of the brothers at the same time. Most of whom are still living, though some have fallen asleep. Then he appeared to James, then to all the apostles, and last of all he appeared to me also, as to one abnormally born."[3]

He claimed that the historical resurrection of Jesus from the dead on the third day was verified by his appearances to hundreds of people, who were alive to authenticate their experiences. The tomb was empty, no one could produce the body (and the authorities were undoubtedly trying to locate it), the disciples were transformed from being fainthearted to being fearless, and they changed their day of worship from the time-honored, sacred Sabbath of the seventh day, to the first day of the week, the day of resurrection.

How does seeing the reality of the resurrection of Jesus as a fact of history affect us today? It makes unique claims for the importance of Christ. "Jesus may have been a good teacher or a powerful prophet, but if he was not resurrected, he was at best a moral exemplar like other teachers or prophets. If he has not overcome mortality, he could not lead others to a share of life greater than the merely mortal. If Jesus is not raised, Christianity is simply another cult or ethical society, and not a particularly attractive one. The same is just as true today. Those contemporary forms of Christianity that focus only on the humanity of Jesus believe in vain. They have, sadly, capitulated to the mind of the Enlightenment.... If religion can hold as true only what is 'within the bounds of reason,' and if 'reason' is defined in terms of the empirically verifiable, then the resurrection is excluded by definition. But if the resurrection is excluded, why should Christians continue to revere Jesus, who is then only one of many figures from antiquity worthy of attention and honor? If Jesus is only the 'historical Jesus,' then Christianity is a delusion and a waste of time. But if Jesus is raised as Lord, everything changes radically."[4] He calls us to follow him and confess him as our Master and Lord.[5] He calls us to receive the Spirit that raised him from the dead so that we too may experience resurrection life.[6]

There are many theories of the after-life. Reincarnation is in vogue. Interest in New Age and the occult is booming. The media portrays fictitious accounts of those who die and live on, or come back to earth in a different form. Suicide bombers are guaranteed entry into Paradise by their martyrdom. There is a deep desire to perpetuate oneself as a counter to nihilism. What should we believe?

I first experienced death in my family when I was twelve years of age. My beloved grandmother died suddenly. One day she was alive, and then next day she was dead. I found it hard to believe it could happen. How can life that is so significant be exterminated? There is an illogicality about the extinction of life. Can something so important simply disappear?

The Bible tells us 'no'! The book of Daniel records, "Multitudes who sleep in the dust of the earth will wake; some to everlasting life, others to shame, and everlasting contempt. Those who are wise will shine like the brightness of the heavens, and those who lead many to righteousness, like the stars for ever and ever."[7]

Jesus said, "I am the resurrection and the life. He who believes in me will live, even though he dies; and whoever lives and believes in me will never die."[8]

What does it mean to live and believe in Jesus? It means following him, seeking first his direction for our lives. It means opening our lives to him and his Spirit, so that he lives in us and through us every moment of every day. It means coming to his Cross to seek forgiveness and the strength to change your life for the better. It means trusting in Christ for this life and the life to come. It means giving up control of your life to Christ – control of your agenda, your ambition, your possessions, and your heart. It means seeking to love God with all your heart and mind and soul and strength, and to love your neighbor as yourself. It means being like Jesus, seeking his strength and guidance to be a witness to the truth, and, like him, humbling oneself in order to serve others.

It is simply to live and believe in Jesus, if you are willing to die to self-centeredness, and live into a new life.

Two years after my grandmother died my search for an answer to the questions raised by her death led me to invite the risen Christ into my life. That resulted in many changes in my life. When Jesus rose from the dead on the third day he changed the world. From then on no one could look at life or death the same way.

When walking on the beach at sunrise a beam of light shines directly at me as I look at the sun. Wherever I walk, the sun reaches out to me and follows me. As I walk from south to north along the beach, on one side the sunlight shines on me, and on the other side my shadow stretches out across the sand. I can walk forward indifferent to the sun. I can look at the shadow side. Or I can face into the sun as it pours its golden rays on to me. My decision at age fourteen was to turn toward the Risen Son of God and follow his light.

Jesus said, "I am the light of the world, he who follows me will not walk in darkness, but will have the light of life."[9] That promise has never failed.

24

HE ASCENDED INTO HEAVEN

"To complete your seamless robe, and so to complete our faith, you ascended through the air into the heavens, before the very eyes of the apostles. In this way you showed that you are Lord of all, and are the fulfillment of all creation. Thus from that moment every human and every living creature should bow at your name. And, in the eyes of faith, we can see that all creation proclaims your greatness."[1]

Thus prayed St. Bernard of Clairvaux in the eleventh century. He is referring to St. Luke's account of the Ascension at the end of his Gospel and in the first chapter of Acts. "He was taken up before their very eyes, and a cloud hid him from their sight. They were looking intently up into the sky as he was going, when suddenly two men dressed in white stood beside them. 'Men of Galilee,' they said, 'why do you stand here looking into the sky? This same Jesus, who has been taken from you into heaven, will come back in the same way you have seen him go into heaven.'"[2]

The other gospel writers indicate that Jesus gave them warning of his return to heaven. He told

Mary Magdalene on Easter morning outside the tomb, "Do not hold on to me, for I have not yet returned to the Father. Go instead to my brothers and tell them, 'I am returning to my Father and your Father, to my God and your God.'"[3]

This exaltation of Jesus to the presence of the Father establishes his authority. The cloud symbolizes the shekinah glory[4] with the people of Israel in their travels through the wilderness, and in the Tabernacle, and on the mount of Transfiguration – the visible manifestation of God's presence, glory and approval.[5] Human nature in the form of the body of Jesus is carried into heaven to prepare a place for us.[6] "We have this hope as an anchor for the soul, firm and secure. It enters the inner sanctuary behind the curtain, where Jesus, who went before us, has entered on our behalf."[7]

Jesus, who came down from heaven,[8] accompanied by angels at his birth, returned to heaven with the same heavenly witnesses. He who entered into time from eternity, and was eternally present with the Father, departed from time in this fashion. In his place he sent the Spirit.

This raises the issue of the relationship of Time to Eternity. The Ascension does not mean that Jesus has exited the universe, or that heaven has no connection with earth. All Time is Present to God so that he sees us at every moment of our lives as being Present to him.

C.S. Lewis gives us a picture of Time as a straight line on a page which is God. Time is the line, God is the whole page on which the line is drawn. History occurs in a linear fashion. One thing happens after another. We cannot experience the present until we leave the past. God in eternity is the context in which all Time takes place.

    This analogy is helpful in dealing with the seeming paradox that Jesus can be God in eternity and man in Time at the same moment. We think that God had to suspend his divinity in order to become man, that he saw his time on earth as future before it happened, and then past when it occurred. But God is beyond space and time. He has no history. There can be no past and future with him. He sees everything as present.

    That is why he knows each one of us from before the creation of the world, and to our eternal destiny. Such knowledge does not determine our decisions. He can see ahead and we cannot. Because God is outside Time, he sees everything as present, so that he sees what we call tomorrow in the same way as he sees today. Everything is 'Now' for him. He sees us at each stage in our lives as present to him. He knows what we do in the future because he is already there.[9]

    So that when Jesus said to the thief on the cross that "today you will be with me in paradise,"[10] he was expressing the reality, that death ushers us into eternity. When we leave time at our death, we enter into eternity. There is no conflict between the truth that the resurrection and judgment has to wait until the end of time, and the reality that there is no waiting in eternity. Both occur at the end of history, but our history ends at our death. So we do not have to wait for resurrection, for we are outside time with God.

    Jesus, when he was in Time, had a history. By leaving Time and entering again into eternity he is always Present to us. He has all eternity to listen to our prayers in Time. By removing his physical presence he made himself available to the whole world instantaneously.

Ruth Etchells expressed this truth in her prayer for Ascension Day.

"My Lord Jesus Christ, I do not really begin to understand the mystery of your Ascension, or how to picture it. Only I know that there had to be a time when your physical presence must be withdrawn, for the wider world to encounter your love. And I know that my tender and suffering Lord, and even my victoriously risen and observable Lord, must become the aweful and glorious Lord, King beyond time and space, ruling over all the worlds that are and are to be. And I understand that at your Ascension you went through the door between time and eternity.

"Only, Lord, I should be full of a sense of loss, if it were not for being with your disciples as they return to Jerusalem, not sad, but full of a great joy, bursting into hymns praising God. So Lord, it seems they do not so much see you leaving them, as taking up your rule over all the unacknowledged bits of their lives, including their wonderings about eternity. They show such a profound sense of wondering certainty, Lord, an absoluteness of commitment, devotion and worship.

"So, Lord, like them I return to the city. Fill me too with awe and praise as you take up your kingly rule: renew within me the wonder of Ascension Day discipleship. Amen."[11]

25

HE IS SEATED AT THE RIGHT HAND OF GOD THE FATHER ALMIGHTY

The Empire of Japan unconditionally surrendered at the end of World War Two on August 14, 1945, five days after atomic bombs had been dropped on Hiroshima and Nagasaki. The United States had been at war with Japan since her surprise attack on Pearl Harbor on December 7, 1941. It is believed that 45 million people may have died in the war. But on that August day in 1945 the Allies were victorious over their enemies. There was rejoicing in the streets. In one of the earliest memories I have as a child in New Zealand, I can remember my mother giving me a gong that was rung to announce that dinner was served, to take out into the street and ring to my heart's content. Vulnerable as we were to the Japanese advance into the south Pacific we were so relieved that we no longer had to fear danger to ourselves and our loved ones. Our enemies and all that they stood for had been defeated. We, and all that we believed and held sacred, had won. There was dancing in the streets and partying into the night. We woke up the next morning to a world at peace – the first time for six years. It took a while to grow accustomed to the change.

We had been at war for so long – all my lifetime – that it was hard to adjust to the fact that victory had been won – at great cost – but won.

It is that kind of reaction which we are meant to experience when we affirm in the Apostles' Creed that we believe that Jesus Christ is seated at the right hand of God the Father Almighty. The right hand of God is the place of supreme honor reserved for the conquering hero. He is given authority to rule over every other power because he has defeated his enemies. This picture of Jesus Christ sitting at the right hand of God runs right through almost the whole New Testament. It is in the first Christian sermon by Peter in Jerusalem at Pentecost.[1] He proclaims it to the religious council of the Sanhedrin.[2] It is in the dying vision of Stephen.[3] Jesus prophesied that the day would come when they would see him at the right hand of God.[4] Paul writes about it many times.[5] The phrase runs all through the New Testament. Let me take but one of them from 1 Cor.15:24-26

"Then the end will come, when he hands over the kingdom to God the Father after he has destroyed all dominion, authority and power. For he must reign until he has put all his enemies under his feet. The last enemy to be destroyed is death."

Who are his enemies? They are anything that opposes his work of salvation, anything that diminishes life in all its fullness, anything that is touched by death. Where has he defeated them? On the Cross and in the Resurrection. At great cost to himself "having disarmed the powers and authorities, he made a public spectacle of them, triumphing over them by the cross."[6]

We are meant to rejoice because we can live as victors enjoying life in the kingdom of heaven. He has won the victory, and is winning it every day as we join with him in defeating these enemies in our own lives.

What are these enemies and how do we apply his victory over them? The enemies of salvation are the enemies of faith, hope and love. War is fought to protect the security, liberty and justice we deem necessary in order to live. Faith, hope and love are the values Christ calls us to fight for in the war on his enemies, the war for the kingdom of heaven. He has won the victory, but we must adjust to that victory and live into what it has secured for us.

If we are fighting for faith we must attack anxiety with confidence, and confront fear with the assurance that Christ has won the battle, and that we must trust in him. If we are threatened by death and hell we must be protected by the promise of eternal life and heaven. When we experience suffering in the battle, we must offer it up as part of the cost of salvation, knowing that in the Cross we will be ultimately healed and vindicated.

If we are fighting for hope, we must resist surrendering to despair because we know that all eventually will be well, and that "we are more than conquerors through him who loved us."[7] When cynicism tempts us, we will learn to rise above it, when skepticism assails us, we will use the weapon of affirmation, reminding ourselves of all that we have and are given in Christ.

If we are fighting for love, we will defeat selfishness with generosity, envy with appreciation, arrogance with humility, irritability with patience, rudeness with kindness, harshness with gentleness.

How do we do this? How do we enjoy and experience the victory of Christ over his enemies, the victory of faith, hope and love?

It is a question of power. Not military power but spiritual power. Paul writes about God's "incomparably great power for us who believe. That power is like the working of his mighty strength, which he exerted in Christ when he raised him from the dead and seated him at his right hand in the heavenly realms.... And God raised us up with Christ and seated us with him in the heavenly realms."[8] We have been given a share in the victory of Christ. Therefore, we are called to "set your hearts on things above, where Christ is seated on the right hand of God."[9]

To "set your heart" on something is to long for it, to desire to acquire it, to possess it. If our destination, our goal, is heaven, then we must be training ourselves to live in heaven. If we want to live in that new world, we must be preparing for our citizenship in heaven. That means acquiring the skills to defeat the enemies of the kingdom of heaven by practicing the values of heaven now. It means drawing on the power of Christ through prayer, and worship, and discipleship, to win the victory in our lives every day.

"When the Son of Man comes in his glory, and all the angels with him, he will sit on his throne in heavenly glory. All the nations will be gathered before him, and he will separate the people one from another as shepherd separates the sheep from the goats. He will put the sheep on his right [the place of honor and victory] and the goats on his left."[10]

What are the criteria for the division between the sheep and goats, the right hand and the left hand of the Son of Man? It is how we treated Christ, how we followed him, how we responded to his presence in our lives as we encountered others. It is how we lived out the victory of Christ in our relationships with one another. It is how we lived into the truths and values the war he fought was meant to secure. It is how we embodied in our behavior the characteristics of the kingdom of heaven.

We are given the power to do this by the Gospel of Jesus. "It is the power of God for the salvation of everyone who believes."[11] The Gospel makes it possible for us goats to be transformed into sheep. The power of Jesus, when called on, enables people to be changed from the left to the right hand side of God. His incomparably great power for us who believe turns enemies into allies. Corrie ten Boom used to say, "Jesus is Victor." When we realize this and live into it day by day, we can rejoice that the war is won. He has put all his enemies under his feet.

26

HE SHALL COME TO JUDGE THE QUICK AND THE DEAD

Jesus comes in various ways to us in our lifetime. He comes in His Word and Sacraments. He comes into our lives by his Holy Spirit. He comes in the presence of others. He comes through the events, the crises and celebrations, of life. He comes back to take us to be with him in the place he has prepared for us when we die. There are many comings of Christ. But the Creed calls us to affirm our belief in his coming at the end of time, when he will judge the world. This belief that Jesus will come again as Judge of the world is an integral part of the Gospel in the New Testament.

Peter testified that Jesus "Commanded us to preach to the people and to testify that he is the one whom God appointed as judge of the living and the dead."[1] Paul told the Athenians that God "has set a day when he will judge the world with justice by the man he has appointed. He has given proof of this to all men by raising him from the dead."[2] He reminded the Corinthians: "For we must all appear before the judgment seat of Christ, that each one may receive what is due him for the things done while in the body, whether good or bad."[3]

The Scriptures teach that there is rarely ultimate justice in this life. John Pearson, writing on this article of the Creed in 1659 put it this way. "The wicked and disobedient persons are often so happy, as if they were rewarded for their impieties; the innocent and religious often so miserable, as if they were punished for their innocency. Nothing more certain, than that in this life rewards are not correspondent to the virtues, punishments not proportionable to the sins, of men. Which consideration will enforce one of these conclusions; either that there is no judge of the actions of mankind; or if there be a judge, he is not just, he renders no proportionate rewards or punishments; or lastly, if there be a judge, and that judge be just, then there is judgment in another world, and the effects thereof concern another life."[4]

Discussion about the final judgment is complicated by how it has been presented. We have been repulsed by the way some preachers have been preoccupied by this article of the Creed and given it prominence out of all proportion. They create a scenario of hellfire and brimstone, and lay on guilt, in order to manipulate their hearers. Such an approach takes a truth about accountability and makes it the *only* truth about life and God. At the other end of the spectrum are those who present the grace and love of God as irresistible and all-forgiving, requiring no repentance or reparation on the part of evildoers. Where does the balanced and full truth lie?

Pearson gives the following three reasons to believe in a universal judgment:

First, a belief that God is just and holy requires that there be rewards and punishments in the life to come. Life would be unjust otherwise. Evil has to receive its due sentence and finally be defeated.

Secondly, the prospect of a judgment to come is meant to lead us to repentance, to faith in the Savior's atonement for our sins, and to reformation of character. If there were no other judgment than our own, we would excuse ourselves and be unconcerned about our conscience. But if we all have to give an account of our actions or inactions, what we have done or failed to do "on the day when God will judge men's secrets through Jesus Christ,"[5] we will do something about it now. We are each responsible for how we have lived our lives, and how we have sought forgiveness.

Thirdly, "if we look upon the judgment to come, only as revealing our secrets, as discerning our actions, as sentencing our persons according to our works done in the flesh, there is not one of us can expect life from that tribunal, or happiness at the last day...It is necessary therefore that we should believe, that Christ shall sit upon the throne, that our Redeemer shall be our judge, that we shall receive our sentence not according to the rigour of the Law, but the mildness and mercies of the Gospel."[6] The Judge is also our Savior and High-Priest who lives to make intercession for us. "I tell you the truth, whoever hears my word and believes him who sent me has eternal life and will not be condemned; he has crossed over from death to life."[7]

Alister McGrath[8] suggests that being judged by Christ should not be threatening. "First of all we are being judged by someone who knows us totally. We need not fear a superficial judgment, based on inadequate knowledge of us and our situation. God knows us totally[9] and loves us still. This should be a reassuring thought. We can be honest about ourselves with God." He knows the real you and me.

Secondly, "we are being judged by someone who is passionately committed to us. We are being judged by someone who cares for us" and who is sympathetic toward us.

Thirdly, "we are judged by someone whom we know and trust. We are already judged by our attitudes toward Jesus. We are not judged on the basis of something unknown, but on our response to Jesus coming to us. Our attitude toward Jesus determines our attitude toward God. That judgment is confirmed at the last day." We make the decision by which we are judged. If we are trusting in Jesus and seeking to respond to his guidance in our lives we will find mercy and grace at the last.

Some theologians suggest that the believer in Christ has two kinds of judgments. The first is the judgment of salvation, in which the criteria is how we respond to the grace of God in Christ through the gift of faith. The second is the judgment based on our works, or life, after we have trusted in Christ for our salvation.

The first, recounted to me by Fitz Allison in a personal letter, is exemplified by the conversion experience of Charles Wesley. "Peter Bohler asked Charles on his sick bed what confidence he had when facing the judgment of God. "That I have given my best endeavors to serve the Lord," was his pre-conversion response. Peter then gave him Martin Luther's commentary on the Epistle to the Galatians, and halfway through Charles gave up his self-righteous burden for the "yoke of Christ" and his easy burden. It was then that 8,000 hymns began to pour from his broken and newborn heart. It was in no confidence that he had done well enough to be saved. "Well enough" was as filthy rags before God. The mercy found in Christ was the confidence of this converted sinner, Charles Wesley."

The second kind of judgment – on how we have lived while trusting in Christ and his grace - may be seen in the story of Russell Conwell. In *Shields of Brass*, Roy Angell wrote that the editor of a newspaper sent well-known writer Bruce Barton to the hospital to talk to Russell Conwell. Conwell, a Baptist clergyman, founder of Philadelphia's Temple University, and author of the world-famous classic *Acres of Diamonds*, was critically ill.

Barton told Conwell that all the world knew about his great work and his famous lecture, "Acres of Diamonds," which he had delivered hundreds of times. But, Barton said, he had been sent to find out if Conwell had any fear as he came to the close of his life.

Conwell hesitated for a few minutes and then told Barton that as a boy of fourteen on a New England farm he learned an unforgettable lesson.

"One day my dad called me into the house and told me that he had to go into town to take care of some business and that he would be gone a day or so. He said the bottom land needed to be plowed, and that some of the cattle had broken through the fence and they needed to be brought back and the fence needed to be fixed. He said that the wagon needed to be greased so that they could use it upon his return to haul corn to the market."

Then Conwell said that as his father left he said to his son, "Do the best you can."

"The next night I dragged into the house bone tired just as my dad returned from town. The first thing he wanted to know was how I had made out in his absence," Conwell said.

"I got them all done," Conwell said with pride.

"You got them all done?" his father asked. "Did you get the bottom land plowed? Are the cows back in the field and is the fence fixed? Did you get the wagon greased? That's a whole lot of work, son. Do you mean you got it all done?" the elder Conwell asked.

"Beaming with pride, I said, "Yes, Father, I got them all done."

Then Russell Conwell said his dad looked straight at him and said, "A good day's work, Russ."

Conwell continued, "Bruce," he said, "Before long my Heavenly Father and I are going to meet face to face. I think He will put his arm around me and say to me, 'Son, you've done a good day's work; a good day's work.'"

Barton said he tiptoed out of the room feeling that he had stood on holy ground.[10]

We prepare for the judgment day by welcoming Jesus Christ into our lives, by trusting in his righteousness and not our own, by living each day as though it were our last, and by doing all the good we can, as he directs and enables us. It is Christ who gives us the ability to be good and faithful servants. We are commended in the judgment day insofar as we have responded to his grace with the faith that produces works of love. As Fitz Allison reminded me, "The treasure to be found is that God's costly love in Christ has established mercy for the grossly inadequate duties we each have performed in this life."

I BELIEVE IN THE HOLY SPIRIT

Today there is more interest than ever in the person and work of the Holy Spirit. In Africa, Asia, and Latin America it is churches that emphasize the work of the Holy Spirit that are growing. They take the need for the power and gifts of the Holy Spirit as essential in order for their ministry to be effective. Michael Green in his memoir, *Adventure of Faith*, writes of the church of Southeast Asia: "They live with a profound awareness of the Holy Spirit of God, and they seek to draw him into everything they do. They consciously seek to keep in step with the Spirit."[1]

Paul writes about the conflict between the Spirit-centered nature in each individual Christian believer and the self-centered nature. It is the task of discipleship to defeat, or subdue the self-centered nature by the Spirit-centered nature. He concludes that to live by the Spirit, is to "keep in step with the Spirit."[2] Marching, or walking with the Spirit, at the same pace, in the same direction, without being chronically hobbled by the self-centered nature, is a description of the Christian life.

To believe in the Holy Spirit means to live one's life by the Spirit of God, who is the Spirit of Christ. To believe in the Holy Spirit is to ask our Father in heaven for the gift of the Spirit.[3] To believe in the Holy Spirit is to show his gifts and fruit in our actions.

There is a tendency in Christian churches and in individual experience to focus on one person of the Holy Trinity and to neglect the other two. Some churches talk about God and emphasize the Fatherhood of God. Nowadays, even Fatherhood is being replaced in some churches by gender-neutral terms such as Creator. Most of these churches are liberal in their theology, and want to be as inclusive as possible. Other churches emphasize God the Son, and are Christ-centered, with the focus on salvation, justification, and the Cross. Most of these churches are evangelical and conservative in their theology. Then there are those churches that emphasize the Holy Spirit, miracles, healing, and spiritual experience. They are Pentecostal, or main-line charismatic churches. You can find your own orientation by checking out how you pray, to whom you pray, and what you pray for.

It is desirable for us to be Trinitarian in our focus so that we do not neglect worship of any member of the Godhead. Churches or individuals who fail to appreciate the ministry of each Person will be deficient in their experience. The Creed reminds us that the Holy Spirit is necessary for our life.

On the day of Pentecost, the Spirit of God came with power upon the apostles. "Without warning there was a sound like a strong wind, gale force – no one could tell where it came from. It filled the whole building. Then, like a wildfire, the Holy

Spirit spread through their ranks, and they started speaking in a number of different languages as the Spirit prompted them."[4]

The word for Holy Spirit in the Bible is *wind*, or *breath*. In Hebrew it is *ruach*, in Greek it is *pneuma*. It was the Spirit of God who was hovering over the waters in the beginning of creation, and formed man from the dust of the ground by breathing into his nostrils the breath of life.[5] Jesus said to Nicodemus: "The wind blows where it wishes; you hear the sound it makes, but you do not know where it comes from or where it is going. It is like that with everyone who is born of the Spirit."[6] The Holy Spirit makes us living beings at the beginning of life, and also remakes us when he regenerates us in Christ.

God's action is like the wind, strong, boisterous, uncontrollable. When he comes into our lives he disturbs us. Just as the wind shakes the trees and rattles the shutters, makes waves, and rocks the boat, the wind of God can shake us up, and rearrange our lives. The Spirit of God can cause agitation and discomposure. The Holy Spirit is God at work in our world. His goal is to bring life, new life into the world. He takes ordinary people and changes them into vehicles of his purpose in the lives of others. Gideon was a very ordinary man until the Spirit of God took possession of him. Samson had mighty strength because the Spirit of the Lord came mightily upon him.

The Holy Spirit not only changes people, he changes situations. He not only brings new life but also new opportunities. Moses and the Israelites were trapped between the Egyptian army and the Red Sea when "the Lord drove the sea back with a strong east wind. It blew all night and turned the sea into dry land."[7] The Holy Spirit created a way forward that nobody envisaged. When you think that all is over – that there is nowhere for you to go, no answer to your problems, then the invading force of the Holy Spirit can create an unexpected way forward.

Ezekiel was set down in the valley of dry bones and the Lord joined the bones together and said to him, "Mortal man, prophesy to the wind. Tell the wind that the Sovereign Lord commands it to come from every direction to breathe into these dead bodies and to bring them back to life. Breath entered the bodies and they came to life and stood up." [8] When everything seems finished, when there is no hope, the Holy Spirit breathes new life, and creates new beginnings.

This is God in action, the wind of the Holy Spirit roaring through the world, changing lives. But we try to organize and domesticate the Holy Spirit. Can you control the wind? No. "The wind blows wherever it wishes." This is God we are dealing with. We forget that God does not only speak in a gentle whisper, but also in a boisterous bellow.

Mary Ellen Ashcroft, in her delightful allegory of the Gospel, *Dogspell, A Dogmatic Theology on the Abounding Love of God*, has a chapter on *Your Dog Is Too Small (Let Go and Let Dog)*.

"Institutions try to be practical, responsible. In Acts 1 the guys gather for an important subcommittee meeting. 'Let's see, Jesus said to wait, so what shall we do? He couldn't have meant just wait. I guess we're short of one of the twelve; so let's elect a new one, how 'bout, and that'll get things ready to go.' God confounds them, chuckling as Spirit bowls them over. Gale-force wind, a fire raging out of control, a torrential downpour of languages: Luke's best effort to describe Pentecost. The tiny match catches, and soon it is a wall of flame, crackling sparks fly off the top, billows of smoke. Of course you can't pour a cup of water on it or throw a blanket over it. Run for your life! Onlookers can only conclude the disciples are drunk – they're so noisy and high-spirited.

"The church has tried desperately to domesticate the Spirit. 'Sit.' 'You can't do it that way. No, you have to be converted first and then receive the Spirit.' 'Stay.' 'The Spirit's role is to convict you of sin.' 'Roll over.' 'The Spirit was necessary before the canon of Scripture was complete.' 'Heel.'

"God delighted, God reckless – the generous luxury of God, incongruous with religious experience. The Spirit is unpredictable – living water overflowing banks, waterfalls washing, flooding. Alpine meadows teeming with flowers, bees, butterflies, grace upon grace. Drenched in spirit, flowing over, around and through you, making you dance as you never thought you could. You shout, you run, you hug, you tango. Someone lets dog in (or out), and she joins, leaping, licking, wagging, romping, frolicking.

"The Spirit is embarrassing. Pentecost is like a Down's syndrome child, speaking in a full voice at a concert, 'I'm having such a good time. I'm very happy.' Pentecost is the one-year-old flapping arms and legs when Dad walks in. Someone needs to teach these folks moderation. Help 'em to not show so much emotion; teach them some manners, for heaven's sake.

"The church dreads Pentecost, miracles, apparitions. Church authorities hope against hope that no one will see an appearance of Mary. What a nuisance all these uneducated peasants, expecting to encounter the divine. They won't take no for an answer.

"Neither will the divine. Over and over God does the unexpected, making himself unpopular with the church offices who have spiritual life in neat files until God comes along. Enthusiasm, Bishop Butler suggested to John Wesley, is a terrible thing, a very terrible thing.

'I beg to differ,' says God. Enthusiasm, dog knows, is at the heart of love, carrying you away so that you can't help but wag. Pentecost is a dance of greeting: the whole body wags, a wiggle of warmth."[9]

It is an illusion to think that we are in control of our lives, yet most of us go to great lengths to persuade ourselves and others that we are. We want God and life on our own terms, in neat packages, so that we are not overwhelmed, or feel insecure. When the circumstances of our lives appear more out of control than normal, we do everything in our own power to correct things. But we try to do our best in our own strength. We try to get everything back under control, so that we can manage our lives. We end up experiencing a great deal of stress, and developing life-threatening physical symptoms. Stephen said, "How stubborn you are! How heathen your hearts, how deaf you are to God's message! You are just like your ancestors; you too have always resisted the Holy Spirit."[10] We can be so stubborn, so unbelieving, so uptight about life, we refuse to bend with the wind of the Holy Spirit. If we surrender to the power of the Holy Spirit, we might see some miracles happening.

To believe in the Holy Spirit is to believe in a dynamic, powerful God who gives us life, and wants

The Holy Spirit

to continue to give us new life in Christ. He invites us to choose to live by the Spirit.

We are invited to be led by the Spirit, to follow the guidance of the Spirit, rather than to be led by the contemporary culture.

We are encouraged to be filled by the Spirit, so that you may grow the fruit of the Spirit: love, joy, peace, patience, kindness, goodness, faithfulness, gentleness and self-control.

We are given the gifts of the Spirit to use in ministry to others: wise counsel, clear understanding, simple trust, healing the sick, miraculous acts, distinguishing between spirits, tongues, interpretation of tongues, preaching, teaching, encouraging, serving, giving, leading, administering, showing mercy and others.

We are urged to seek to be filled by the Spirit daily so that we might keep in step with the Spirit. We are encouraged to pray that God might strengthen us with power through his Spirit in our inner being so that we might overflow with hope.[11]

THE HOLY, CATHOLIC CHURCH

Arthur McKinstry, the father of one of my congregants in Orange Park, and former Episcopal Bishop of Delaware, told me about a meeting he had with Alfred DuPont during World War II. Alfred's wife, Jessie Ball Dupont, was a faithful Episcopalian but her husband was not much of a churchgoer. He told McKinstry that he didn't feel that the church was necessary for him, and that he could be a good person without it. McKinstry said that if that were the case that we should call up President Roosevelt and tell him to disband the armed forces. DuPont was startled, and asked why? McKinstry said, "We don't need the army to fight the war. Just arm each individual citizen and let him get on with the job of fighting Hitler in his own way." Dupont took his point.

The church is necessary to support individual believers and to provide communities with the organization and inspiration to forward God's work. Cyprian of Carthage once wrote, "No one can have God as his father, who does not have the church for his mother." When we acknowledge God as our Father, we join a family with brothers and sisters of the same faith.

In 1942 C.S. Lewis described Christians as living in 'enemy territory.' When much of Europe was occupied by Nazi armies, Lewis suggested that the Church was like a resistance movement that was fighting an invading power of evil. The invading power is determined to defeat and destroy any resistance to its authority. God provided the church to organize his followers in resistance.

Throughout history there has been a continuous battle between the forces of evil and the kingdom of God. The Church is one of God's weapons in that battle. The German and Scottish words for church are 'kirche', and 'kirk'. They are derived from the Greek, 'kurike', which means 'belonging to the Lord.' To belong to the Church is to belong to the Lord Jesus Christ. If we profess Jesus to be our Lord, we will want to belong to his church.

The French and Spanish words for church are 'eglise', and 'iglesia.' They are derived from the Greek, 'ekklesia' which means 'called out.' It is used to describe the calling out of citizens in a town to make decisions. It is the word used to describe the congregation of the people of God called out of Egypt. It tells us that our primary purpose as the Church is to respond to God's call to be his people and to serve him in the world.

Peter puts it this way, "But you are a chosen people, a royal priesthood, a holy nation, a people belonging to God, that you may declare the praises of him who called you out of darkness into his wonderful light."[1]

Peterson translates it: "But you are the ones chosen by God, chosen for the high calling of priestly work, chosen to be a holy people, God's instruments to do his work and speak out for him, to tell others of the night and day difference he made for you."[2]

The basic meaning of 'holy' is 'marked off,' 'separate,' 'set apart' for God's use. It tells us that the church does not belong to itself; it is not its own property. It is not ours to dispose of and to arrange according to our wishes. Its only owner is God, and we are warned about having proprietorial attitudes to the church. We should always be seeking to know what God would have us to do in his church, not just what we want to do.

Our primary purpose is to bear witness in the world to God and to his grace in Jesus Christ in our lives. We are meant to be the light of the world. We witness to what God has done for us – he has pardoned us and made us holy, even though we are undeserving sinners. We are called to become holy in character as he is holy, and so be different from the world and the culture in which we live.

When Jesus told Simon son of Jonah that his name would be Peter, which means 'rock', and that "on this rock I will build my church."[3] he was referring to the fact that it would be Peter's leadership, and proclamation of the Gospel on the day of Pentecost in Jerusalem, that would launch the church on its destiny. All churches descend from that beginning. All churches depend on that apostolic succession, not just those who claim to be successors of Peter, or who think that an unbroken laying on of hands by bishops is a guarantee of legitimacy as the church. When we say that we believe in the 'catholic' church, we are affirming that our congregation is part of this one universal church.

We value our continuity with the church of past ages, and throughout the world. The church is one because we are built upon one foundation, Jesus Christ. The church is universal because it is open to all who respond to the call of Christ whatever their race, ethnicity, language or gender. Christ is the Lord and Savior of all. The church is a world-wide entity not confined by denomination or nationality. We learn from one another, and we support one another wherever the church may be. There is no place for exclusivity or for claims of superiority of one church over another. Where there is too much pride in one's ecclesiastical tradition, there is not enough catholicity. To be catholic is to have sympathies with all; to be broad-minded, not narrow-minded, to be committed to the whole truth.

The following appeared in The Presbyterian Journal, July 7 and 14, 1982:

Why Do I Need Church?

Why can't I worship alone out in the woods, just me and God and the pine trees? Why can't I meet God at the water's edge, wiggling my toes in the warm sand with nothing around me but thousands of sun worshippers?

Why? Because church is a **staff meeting** and Jesus Christ has called us to be a team and to meet with him. Christ is head of the Church, and I wouldn't feel a part of the staff at all if I weren't there; and I'd be little use to the team.

I need church because it's a **court hearing**. There are things I've done wrong this week and the Lord knows it. He wants a chance to straighten me out. I'm accountable to the Judge of all life for my actions.

I need church because it's a **family reunion**. Jesus said, "Who is my family? Those who do my will" (Mark 3:33,35). We are a huge family rejoicing with one another, crying with one another, helping one another. We need each other's support. We have to depend on each other.

I need church because it's a **classroom**. I'm preparing for a mission; I'm on an extended course of study. For the rest of my life I'm enrolled in a course of Christian discipleship. I can't miss a week because each week builds on the one before.

I need church because it's a **hideout**. The sanctuary is a place to get away from the 'busyness' of the world. It's a mini-retreat for me. It's a place to relax, to focus my thoughts on things above, to worship God.

I need church because it's a **billboard**. Sunday morning is one time for me to proclaim to everyone in my community that God is supreme in my life. As my neighbors see me get up week after week and go down to the building on the corner, they can tell who has priority in my life. And if all my brothers and sisters are there too, the neighbors may wonder what is going on there that attracts people so regularly.

I need church because it's a **memorial service**. Imagine that I had been in war and one of my buddies in the foxhole with me threw himself on an enemy hand grenade to save me, and it killed him. Then when I returned to the States, I learned that there was to be a memorial service for him in my hometown. Would I miss that service? Of course not! Jesus died for me. It's to honor him that I attend his memorial service. It's to honor him that I remember his death by taking communion.

I need church because it's a **victory celebration**. Jesus left an empty tomb. We can celebrate his resurrection together. If a day a year is set aside for remembering the Armistice, then at least one day a week should be set aside for remembering the greatest victory of all, Jesus' triumph over death and Satan.

Finally, I need church because it's a **fellowship**, a time to spend with my Father. I'm a child of God. God is my loving Father. He's not cold and aloof; He holds me in his arms; he delights to spend time with me, and I want to be there. But He's not just my Father; He's our Father. He has told us that when two or three are gathered together, He is there (Matt.18:20). I love him and wish to obey him, and he has told me not to forsake gathering with other believers (Hebrews 10:25).

Why do I need church? I need church because I'm part of the team; I'm accountable to the Judge; I'm glad to see my family; I have lots to learn; I need to have a retreat; I want to know God's plans. Moreover, I know what my priorities are. I respect Christ's death and am overjoyed by his resurrection, and I want to spend time with my Father and also with other believers.

That's why I need church!

The church is part of the Gospel. It is part of God's plan for the world. That is why it is important to say we believe in the holy, catholic church, and why it is essential that we belong to it, support it, and participate in its life. As John Wesley said, "The Bible knows nothing of solitary religion."

29

THE COMMUNION OF SAINTS

In *The New York Daily News,* October 1, 2001, Mike Lupica wrote, "It is a football Sunday, The Giants' game, their first home game since September 11, is on the television. So this is a day for the brother to remember football things. All days are hard, he says. You just hope tomorrow will hurt a little less, he says. At least the football things make Chris Suhr smile. He is a kid on the Sundays he remembers. His brother Danny is so very much alive.

'I can hear his voice right now,' Chris Suhr said yesterday. 'I hear him wondering why the linebacker wasn't over in the flat where he was supposed to be.... That sort of thing. Crying because one of the Giants would miss an assignment and the other team would score.'

Chris Suhr is twenty-one months a fireman, no longer considered a rookie, in the department's regular rotation now. His brother Danny was with Engine Company 216, out of Williamsburg, Brooklyn. Danny Suhr was one of the first firemen killed on the morning of September 11, on his way with the rest of the company into tower two when someone who had fallen from tower two, or jumped, landed on top of him. Then

Father Mychal Judge, the Fire Department chaplain, was killed after giving Danny Suhr the last rites of the Catholic Church.

We have talked all the time since that day about how firemen and police officers and all the emergency workers are the real heroes of the city. Danny Suhr was always his kid brother's hero, long before he tried to lead everybody into tower two, back when he was No. 90 of James Madison High and No. 90 of the semipro Brooklyn Mariners, and captain of the Fire Department football team until he finally decided he was too old a couple of years ago, a couple of years before he became one of the firemen of the city who died much too young.

'He had that football mentality,' Chris Suhr said. 'Here I come. Rush the building the way you would the quarterback. He was always ready to go. You couldn't block him and you couldn't stop him. A little over six feet, maybe 250, maybe more. A square box of a guy.'

The engine pulled up near tower two and then No. 90 of Madison High, and all his other teams, the square box of a guy, the linebacker who always wanted to be first to the quarterback or the ball, was running to get ahead of the other guys, wanting to be first in, probably thinking this was the fire of all their lives, until a part of the sky fell on him and killed him.

'He was everything on a football field except real fast,' Pudgie Walsh, Danny Suhr's old coach with the Brooklyn Mariners and with the FDNY team said yesterday. 'He had to pick that day to be fast.'

Danny Suhr was fast from the back step of Engine 216 on the eleventh of September. There were people inside who needed him.

'If my brother had somehow known that one of them in the company might have to die, over there trying to save people's lives, he would have said, 'I gotta go,' Chris Suhr said. 'He would have done what he did, called Nancy, and then he would have gone, never really believing this thing could stop him, either.'

'He wanted to save lives,' Chris Suhr said. 'And he did. The guys in his company are alive today because they were trying to give him CPR in the ambulance.'"

Hebrews 11 lists all the heroes of the faith who died serving God. "I do not have time to tell about Gideon, Barak, Samson, Jephthah, David, Samuel and the prophets, who through faith conquered kingdoms, administered justice, and gained what was promised; who shut the mouths of lions, quenched the fury of the flames, and escaped the edge of the sword; whose weakness was turned to strength......the world was not worthy of them....These were all commended for their faith, yet none of them received what had been promised. God had planned something better for us so that only together with us would they be made perfect."[1]

When we say we believe in the Communion of Saints, we are affirming that our relationship with those who have gone before us into the eternal kingdom of God is unbroken. The foundation of the union between us is Jesus Christ, and therefore that union cannot be removed by death. God never forgets his faithful servants. All those mentioned in Hebrews 11 were commended on account of their faith. But they did not receive the promise of Jesus Christ and his resurrection in their lifetime.

God has given us something better. God has a plan for our lives in Christ. That plan provides that the heroes of the faith throughout the ages should not be made perfect apart from those in Christ. Salvation is social; it concerns the whole people of God. We experience it only as part of the whole people of God. The fullness of salvation comes with the completion of God's promise in the kingdom of God. It is what Christ has done that opens the way into the very presence of God for them as well as for us.

What lies beyond death for those in Christ? "You have come to Mount Zion, to the heavenly Jerusalem, the city of the living God. You have come to thousands upon thousands of angels in joyful assembly, to the church of the firstborn, whose names are written in heaven. You have come to God, the judge of all men, to the spirits of righteous men made perfect, to Jesus the mediator of a new covenant, and to the sprinkled blood."[2]

The Communion of Saints is not individualistic. We are part of a fellowship of the redeemed who are pilgrims on a journey to the heavenly Jerusalem, the city of the living God. We join the celestial creation, as well as those whose names are written in the heavenly book of life. We are part of a community of people of faith. Our experience of life in the church on earth is meant to prepare us for the church in heaven. We are being perfected in this life, made holy, set apart, consecrated to God's service. That is the meaning of 'saint.'

Chris Suhr is separated from his brother Danny in this life, but not necessarily in the life to come. If he trusts in Christ, he does not need to be ignorant about those who die, or to grieve like the unbeliever, who has no hope. "We believe that Jesus died and rose again and so we believe that God will bring with Jesus those who have fallen asleep in him."[3]

Holy Communion is a foretaste of the heavenly banquet in which people will come from the east and the west and feast in the kingdom of heaven. It reminds us that our fellowship, our community is based upon our relationship with Jesus Christ, who gives us the promise of eternal life. That promise is sure and rock-solid.

A Prayer.

Eternal God, make us this day to remember the unseen cloud of witnesses who compass about:
>Those who in every age and generation witnessed to their faith in life and in death;
>Those who by their courage and their sacrifice won for us the freedom and liberty we enjoy;
>Those who served their fellow men at the cost of pain, of persecution and of death;
>Those for whom all the trumpets sounded as they passed over to the other side;
>Those whom we have loved and who have gone to be with you,
>and whose names are written on our hearts.

Help us to walk worthily of those in whose unseen presence life is lived. Help us to have in our lives
>Their courage in danger,
>Their steadfastness in trial,
>Their perseverance in difficulty,
>Their loyalty when loyalty is costly,
>Their love which nothing can change,
>Their joy which nothing can take away.

So grant to us in your good time to share with them the blessedness of your nearer presence, that we also may come to that life,
>Where all the questions are answered;
>Where all the tears are wiped away;
>Where we shall meet again, never to be separated

from them, those whom we have loved and lost awhile;
>Where we shall ever be with the Lord.

So grant us in this life never to forget those who have gone before, so that in the life to come we may share their blessedness; through Jesus Christ our Lord. Amen.[4]

30

THE FORGIVENESS OF SINS

Jesus said, "The kingdom of heaven is like a king who wanted to settle accounts with his servants. As he began the settlement, a man who owed him millions of dollars was brought to him. Since he was not able to pay, the master ordered that he and his wife and his children and all that he had be sold to repay the debt."[1]

According to Jesus, God is the ruler to whom we are accountable for our lives. We are in debt to God for life, and love, and health, and everything. He gives us life and can take it away. He holds us responsible for how we live our lives, our stewardship of what opportunities and obligations he has given us. It is not that he is hardhearted or demands more of us than we can do, for he is portrayed as merciful as well as just.

After the servant repents and pledges that he will change his life and repay his master -"The servant's master took pity on him, canceled the debt and let him go." This was at great cost to the king, for he had to write off the debt and absorb the loss.

For anyone who has borrowed money, and been embarrassed when the loan has been called, and they haven't been able to cover it, the experience of forgiveness is rare. But if it were to happen, and all our debts were forgiven we would be so grateful that our lives would be changed for good. But that did not happen to this servant. Jesus tells the story this way: "But when that servant went out, he found one of his fellow servants who owed him a few dollars. He grabbed him and began to choke him. 'Pay back what you owe me!' he demanded. His fellow servant fell on his knees and begged him, 'Be patient with me, and I will pay you back.' But he refused. Instead, he went off and had the man thrown into prison until he could pay his debt."[2] The generosity he had been shown was not extended to his fellow servant who owed him only a few dollars. When the king heard about it, as God does about everything we do or fail to do, he punished him severely by reinstating his debt.

Heinrich Heine said on his deathbed, "God will pardon me. It is his trade." But it would seem that God's forgiveness is conditional. Jesus taught us to pray, "Forgive us our sins, *as* we forgive those who sin against us." The apostle John said that we have to "confess our sins, God is faithful and just to forgive us our sins."[3] Forgiveness is not as easy as it appears. Forgiveness is costly. It requires an awareness of the seriousness of sin, and its remedy.

For many people 'sin' is an outworn word, to be trivialized, and replaced by 'misjudgment' and 'mistake' for which we only need to apologize to make it go away. But there are consequences for sins, just as there are for crimes. Just as there are human laws which are necessary to be obeyed, there are divine laws which carry divine sanctions. The commands of Scripture can be watered down, and regarded as outdated, but they have stood the test of time, and we slight them at our peril. They are the foundation of human relationships, family and society.

They have content and applications which are necessary for a just and loving community.

In the Bible sin means missing the target, the failure to achieve a goal. It also means trespass or transgression, the stepping over a known boundary, and lawlessness, the disregard and violation of known law. An objective criterion is implied, either a standard we fail to reach or a line we deliberately cross. It is assumed throughout Scripture that this criterion or ideal has been established by God. It is his moral law. The source of sin is the self-centeredness and pride of the human heart, and the desire to defy God by going our own way.

The clarity and authority of God's moral law is attacked today by rejecting the divine inspiration of the Scriptures. Instead of the commandments being seen as the Word of God they are described as merely the sanctions primitive tribes, and ancient civilizations adopted in order to maintain order, and punish lawbreakers. Enlightened men and women who have evolved beyond the need for such sanctions are now free to invent and adopt their own standards by which they hold themselves accountable. In which case there is no such category as sin, and no need for forgiveness. In fact, we have discovered so much about genetic conditioning and environmental factors in human development that we cannot always say that we are responsible for our actions. There are those who teach that the Bible simply does not cover what we now know about the human condition, and that the Holy Spirit has led us to new and greater truths that lead us to affirm behavior that previous generations would have condemned as immoral.

Historic Christian theology, would counter this approach by saying that individual responsibility for one's action, or failure to act, is at the heart of the definition of being human. Take away responsibility for one's life, and you take away accountability, the importance of choice, and the ability to execute justice. Without responsibility human beings are reduced to animals, or machines, and life is reduced to the survival of the fittest.

Instead, Jesus tells us we are to be held accountable, and that God, the just and holy God, is also merciful. He came and provided restitution for our sins in the Cross of Christ. He bore the cost of forgiveness so that we might be pardoned, and our lives changed. He wants us to become like him – generous and merciful to others. If we believe in the forgiveness of sins we believe it, not only for ourselves but for others. Our forgiveness is conditional on our being willing to suffer the cost of forgiving others.

If it is hard for us to forgive others, think how hard it must have been for God to forgive us. Charles Allen has two suggestions for us in order to forgive others. "First, take a sheet of paper and across the top write down everything you can remember that you have done wrong. [And that you have failed to do that you should have done.] When you have written down all the wrongs and faults of your life you can remember, put the paper aside but keep thinking, and as additional things come to mind, add them to the list."

"It will be a painful experience. In fact, it will give you a taste of what hell is like. Speaking of hell, Paterson-Smyth wrote:

> And the ghosts of forgotten actions
> Came floating before my sight,
> And the things that I thought were dead things,
> Were alive with a terrible might.

> And the vision of all my past life,
> Was an awful thing to face
> Alone, alone with my conscience,
> In that strange and terrible place.

"When you finish your list, then take another sheet of paper and put down whatever it is you do not want to or feel you cannot forgive in that other person. Then compare the two lists. You will see immediately the point in the story Jesus told of the man who was forgiven a debt of millions of dollars yet refused to forgive another of only a few dollars. You will be so ashamed and you will feel acutely your own need that you will fall on your knees praying, 'God be merciful to me a sinner.' And as you think of your own need of God's forgiveness, you will find it easy to forgive every person you hold anything against."

"My second suggestion for those who find it hard to forgive is, after you have looked carefully at your own sins, lift your eyes away from yourself and 'that other person' and look at Christ...With the picture of your sins and of Him on the cross, forgiveness of others will come within easy reach for you."[4]

If we still find it hard to admit that we need forgiveness, and equally hard to receive it when we do admit it; and if we still desire revenge on those who have hurt us or those whom we love, God reminds us that He is the ultimate Judge, and we must trust in him to do what is right.[5] We can only bow before his authority.

THE RESURRECTION OF THE BODY

The difference between believing in the resurrection of the body and the immortality of the soul is the difference between discovering gold bullion and worthless paper currency of a bankrupt regime. But many people cannot see the difference, and are confused about it. Belief in the immortality of the soul is an ancient Greek hope in the hereafter. The historic Christian faith of the New Testament teaches the resurrection of the body. The ancient Greeks, like the philosopher Plato, generally had a lower view of the body. The goal of philosophy was to set one's mind on the higher things, the Ideal, and so rise above the material body of flesh and blood, so that we might be freed from the prison house of the soul. They believed that after we die, we go to the underworld, the land of 'shades,' where we become fleeting shadows.

When the Scriptures said 'soul,' they were not thinking of some fleeting shadow, they were thinking something akin to our word 'personality,' that is, who we are at our fullest, our deepest selves, our whole being, body and soul, complete selves. Thus, in the resurrection of Jesus, we came to believe in the resurrection of the body.

Jesus, when he was resurrected, appeared to the disciples in bodily form. He was not a ghost. When he departed from them in the ascension, his body disappeared. We are created by God as embodied, mortal creatures, not spirits. "The human soul is not an immortal substance encased in a mortal body. The life of the person (soul) emerges simultaneously with the bodily form of human existence. Human life has no existence independent of a body."[1]

Even in the womb, the psalmist sees that we were given a personal identity by God.[2] What happens when the life of the body has expired? Even as our personal identity was present in the unborn state through God's creation and determination, so we can survive death by that same power and knowledge. So what happens to us when death occurs?

St. Paul puts it this way: "We know that when these bodies of ours are taken down like tents and folded away, they will be replaced by resurrection bodies in heaven – God-made not handmade – and we'll never have to relocate our 'tents' again.... We've been given a glimpse of the real thing, our true home, our resurrection bodies!"[3] Paul doesn't base his belief in the indestructibility of the soul, but on the Spirit of God. There is no suggestion that a 'soul' survives death as a disembodied substance awaiting a spiritual body. It is this mortal body that puts on immortality. "For the perishable must clothe itself with the imperishable, and the mortal with immortality. When the perishable has been clothed with the imperishable, and the mortal with immortality, then the saying that is written will come true: 'Death has been swallowed up in victory.'"[4]

Immortality is gained through resurrection. In 1 Corinthians 15, Paul reminds us that the physical body when it dies is perishable, but "it is raised imperishable; it is sown in dishonor, it is raised in glory; it is sown in weakness, it is raised in power; it is sown a natural body, it is raised a spiritual body."[5] A person is granted immortality, not as disembodied 'soul' but as a whole human person, as a body/soul unity.

Job expresses this hope: "after my skin has been destroyed, yet in my flesh I will see God; I myself will see him with my own eyes – I, and not another."[6] Our personal identity survives in the resurrected body, not a nonphysical entity. We do not have an immortal soul or mind imprisoned in our body. We do not possess immortality by virtue of who we are. Just as we are given natural life in the first place by the grace of God, we are given a resurrection life by the grace of God through the resurrection power of Christ. Our survival after death is not based on some nonphysical aspect of our person but on our relationship to the risen Jesus Christ through the Holy Spirit. "If the Spirit of him who raised Jesus Christ from the dead dwells in you, he who raised Christ from the dead will give life to your mortal bodies also through his Spirit that dwells in you."[7]

The resurrection of our bodies is part of the deliverance of the whole creation. Oscar Cullmann reminds us that the Christian hope relates not only to my individual fate, but to the entire creation.[8] In Romans 8 "Paul writes that the whole creation waits longingly for deliverance. This deliverance will come when the power of the Holy Spirit transforms all matter, when God in a new act of creation will not *destroy* matter, but set it free from the flesh [the sinful nature], from corruptibility. Not eternal Ideas, but concrete objects will then ride anew, in the new, incorruptible life-substance of the Holy Spirit; and among these objects belongs our body as well...It is not a transition from this world to another world, as is the case of the immortal soul freed from the body; rather it is the transition from the present age to the future. It is tied to the whole process of redemption."[9]

"We know that the whole creation has been groaning as in the pains of childbirth right up to the present time. Not only so, but we ourselves, who have the first-fruits of the Spirit, groan inwardly as we wait eagerly for our adoption as sons, the redemption of our bodies. For in this hope we were saved."[10]

"Therefore the Christian belief in the resurrection, as distinct from the Greek belief in immortality, it tied to a *divine total process* implying deliverance. Sin and death must be conquered. *We* cannot do this. *Another* has done it for us; and He was able to do it only in that He betook himself to the province of death – that is, He himself died and expiated sin, so that death as the wages of sin is overcome. Christian faith proclaims that Jesus has done this and that He arose *with* body and soul after He was fully and really dead. Here God has consummated the miracle of the new creation expected at the End. Once again He has created life as in the beginning. At this one point, in Jesus Christ this has already happened! Resurrection, not only in the sense of the Holy Spirit's taking possession of the *inner* man, but also the resurrection of the *body*. This is a new creation of matter, an incorruptible matter. Nowhere else in the world is there this new spiritual matter. Nowhere else is there a spiritual body – only here in Christ.... Even those who believe in the immortality of the soul do not have the hope of which Paul speaks, the hope which expresses the belief of a divine miracle of new creation which will embrace everything, every part of the world created by God. Indeed for the Greeks who believed in the immortality of the soul, it may have been harder to accept the Christian preaching of the resurrection than it was for others...

"The Emperor Marcus Aurelius, the philosopher who belonged with Socrates to the noblest figures of antiquity, also perceived the contrast. As is well known, he had the deepest contempt for Christianity. One might think that the death of the Christian martyrs would have inspired respect in this great Stoic who regarded death with equanimity. But it was just the martyrs' death with which he was least sympathetic. The alacrity with which Christians met their death displeased him. The Stoic departed this life dispassionately; the Christian martyr on the other hand died with spirited passion for the cause of Christ, because he knew that by doing so he stood within a powerful redemptive process. The first Christian martyr, Stephen, shows us (Acts 7:55) how very differently death is bested by him who dies in Christ than by the ancient philosopher: he sees, it is said, 'the heavens open and Christ standing at the right hand of God!' He sees Christ the Conqueror of Death. With this faith that the death he must undergo is already conquered by Him who has Himself endured it, Stephen lets himself be stoned."[11]

Christianity is a material religion. We believe in the worth and value of the body. God gave us our bodies. We cannot imagine anyone without a body. Each of us is some body. As William Willimon writes, "When you lose someone, it's not their disembodied 'spirit,' some vague thing floating above reality for which we grieve. We love their eyes, voice, quirky expressions, and funny little ways of being some body. That graceful wavy hair, that unique tone of voice, that laugh, and touch... We shall see, and know, and take delight."[12]

Willimon states that belief in the resurrection of the body leads us to three ancillary beliefs. "First, since God loves us all, including the body, therefore we need to be good stewards of God's creation by caring for and respecting our bodies. We should not abuse our bodies with over-eating, substance abuse, and a sedentary lifestyle."

"Second, since God loves us distinctly, uniquely, particularly, that is, bodily, we should love one another in the same way. That is why physical affection is so important to us humans. We are created to touch, to embrace, and to communicate our love intimately with one another. We are to value physical affection and to express our love appropriately to the intimacy of our relationship."

"Third, since bodies matter we should be concerned about the physical lives of others. That means being concerned about bodies suffering from abuse, addiction, sickness, famine, war, and disease. Belief in the resurrection of the body, while it gives us hope for the future life, does not give us an excuse to ignore the needs of the present life."

To know and believe that we are going somewhere after this life is another part of the treasure chest of the Gospel of Christ.

32

THE LIFE EVERLASTING

When I was ten years old a movie that made quite an impression on me was *Pandora and the Flying Dutchman*, starring James Mason and Ava Gardner. It was a modern rendition of the legend of the Flying Dutchman, immortalized by Richard Wagner in his opera of that name. Captain Frederick Marryat also wrote about it in his novel, *The Phantom Ship*. The Dutch captain of a sailing ship in the seventeenth century was condemned to live forever after challenging the wrath of God Almighty by swearing a blasphemous oath in the midst of a storm as he attempted to round the Cape of Good Hope. The curse could only be lifted through the love of a woman! So the unfortunate Dutch captain returned to land every seven years in a hopeless search for salvation, because he could only find eternal peace in the arms of a faithful woman.

Belief in life everlasting is not comforting if one is condemned to live out a curse where one can never be fulfilled. Living forever with all one's memories and regrets can be hell. The recent movie, *Groundhog Day*, starring Bill Murray, is another cinematic take on a similar theme: waking up every day and having to repeat the day before.

Malcolm Muggeridge references Jonathan Swift in *Gulliver's Travels* who invented the immortal Stuldbrugs of the flying island of Laputa. Gulliver supposed they would be wise, serene and knowledgeable because of their great age, and instead found them the most miserable of creatures, excruciatingly boring to themselves and to others. Whenever they see a funeral Gulliver learns, they lament and repine that others are gone to a harbor of rest, at which they themselves never can hope to arrive.

Muggeridge, who himself lived to be 87 years of age, wrote: "Indeed, sanely regarded, death may be seen as an important factor in making life tolerable; I like very much the answer given by an octogenarian when asked how he accounted for his longevity – 'Oh, just bad luck!' No doubt for this reason among others, death has often in the past been celebrated rather than abhorred; for instance, very exquisitely by the Metaphysical Poets, among whom John Donne may be regarded as the very lauriate of death. So alluring did he find the prospect of dying that when he was Dean of St. Paul's [Cathedral in London] he had himself painted in his shroud so as to be reminded of the deliverance from life that lay ahead. Sleep, he points out, even just for a night, wonderfully refreshes us; how much more, then, will sleeping into eternity be refreshing! And then:

One short sleep past, we wake eternally,
And Death shall be no more, Death thou shalt die.

In our own time, Dietrich Bonhoeffer manifested a similar attitude to death, when, with his face shining in joyful expectation, he said to the two Nazi guards who had come to take him to be executed: 'For you it is an end, for me a beginning.' Likewise [William] Blake when, on his deathbed, he told his wife Catherine that to him dying was no more than moving from one room to another. As his end approached he sang some particularly beautiful songs, which he told Catherine, were not of his composition, but came directly from heaven."[1]

I have never thought that this life made much sense, logically speaking, unless it was part of a larger existence that transcended this mortal life. Death and human extinction without the prospect of eternal life flies in the face of the value of time, history and God's creation. Muggeridge again,

"There must, in other words, be another reason for our existence and that of the universe, than just getting through the days of our life as best we may; some other destiny than merely using up such physical, intellectual and spiritual creativity as has been vouchsafed us. This, anyway, has been the strongest conviction of the greatest artists, saints, philosophers and, until quite recent times, scientists, through the Christian centuries, who have all assumed that the New Testament promise of eternal life is valid, and that the great drama of the Incarnation which embodies it, is indeed the master drama of our existence. To suppose that these distinguished believers were all credulous fools whose folly and credulity in holding such beliefs has now been finally exposed, would seem to me to be untenable; and anyway I'd rather be wrong with Dante and Shakespeare and Milton, with Augustine of Hippo and Francis of Assisi, with Dr. Johnson, Blake and Dostoevsky, than right with Voltaire, Rousseau, Darwin, the Huxleys, Herbert Spencer, H.G. Wells and Bernard Shaw."[2]

"So like a prisoner awaiting his release, like a schoolboy when the end of term is near, like a migrant bird ready to fly south, like a patient in hospital anxiously scanning the doctor's face to see whether a discharge may be expected, I long to be gone. Extricating myself from the flesh I have too long inhabited, hearing the key turn in the lock of Time so that the great doors of Eternity swing open, disengaging my tired mind from its interminable conundrums and my tired ego from its wearisome insistencies. Such is the prospect of death.

For me, intimations of immortality, deafness, failing eyesight, loss of memory, the afflictions of old age, release me from preoccupation with worldly fantasy and free me to meditate on spiritual reality, to recall Archbishop Fulton Sheen's remark that Christendom is over but not Christ.

And so I live, just for each day, knowing my life will soon be over, and that I, like Michelangelo at the end of his life 'have loved my friends and family. I have loved God and all His creation. I have loved life and now I love death as its natural termination.' [Irving Stone, *The Agony and the Ecstasy*], knowing that although Christendom may be over – Christ lives!"[3]

Jesus spoke much of bringing to us the gift of everlasting, or eternal, life.[4] The New Testament teaches that a living faith in the Son of God grants eternal life.[5] He is the living bread. Anyone who eats him [becomes part of him] will live for ever. "Whoever eats my flesh and drinks my blood has eternal life, and I will raise him up on the last day.... Just as the living Father sent me and I live because of the Father, so the one who feeds on me will live because of me."[6] Identification with Christ in his death and resurrection, by faith, results in sharing in the eternal life of God.

That life is described in poetic terms in the book of Revelation as a "Holy City, the new Jerusalem, coming down out of heaven from God, prepared as a bride beautifully dressed for her husband...There will be no more death or mourning or crying or pain, for the old order of things has passed away."[7]

The Holy City is described in terms of the glory of God: brilliant and colorful like precious jewels, and solid and substantial as a fortress into which no evil can enter. "Nothing impure will ever enter it, nor will anyone who does what is shameful or deceitful, but only those whose names are written in the Lamb's book of life."[8]

It is a place of healing and service,[9] a place of great diversity and interest, because the kings of the earth will bring their splendor into it, and the glory and honor of the nations will be brought into it.[10] The history, beauty, and wisdom of all the world will be represented because of the "great multitude that no one could count, from every nation, tribe, people and language"[11] that inhabits its space.

As a person who enjoys traveling, and reading, and learning about the variety of God's creation, and the history of the world, I would like to imagine that the life everlasting will give me unlimited opportunity to further my knowledge of God and his creation, including my relationships with others. St. Paul tells us that "we will be with the Lord forever."[12]

He reminds us that now "we know in part and we prophesy in part, but when perfection comes the imperfect disappears. When I was a child, I talked like a child, I thought like a child, I reasoned like a child. When I became a man, I put childish ways behind me. Now we see but a poor reflection as in a mirror; then we shall see face to face. Now I know in part; then I shall know fully, even as I am fully known."[13] Love never ends. There is always more to learn and experience about love. And nothing will ever be able to separate us from the love of God that is in Christ Jesus our Lord.[14]

All this means that life everlasting eliminates loneliness and alienation, anxiety and despair, hatred and rejection, failure and regret. In their place we will experience the fullness of life in Christ; the fullness of him who fills all in all. It is joy unspeakable and full of glory. But the fulfillment it brings does not mean boredom or ennui. Penelope Fitzgerald instanced the writing of her uncle, Wilfrid Knox, who maintained that life everlasting would be immensely interesting, because "we should be wrong to think of eternity as static, and, in consequence, boring. Why should we not go on, through all eternity, growing in love and in our power to love."[15]

The tree of life, which was planted by God in the garden of Eden, represents eternal life. After Adam and Eve sinned, God barred access to the tree of life, not as a punishment but as an act of mercy, lest they doom themselves to endless physical life in a fallen world. For us, being barred from the tree of life communicates the truth of the perfection and bliss that the human race lost through its sinfulness. The tree of life is a supreme image of the splendor of the Garden of Eden, and of paradise lost – an image of nostalgia and longing for a lost perfection. But it is also an image of hope to which we look forward. In Revelation the Spirit promises, "To him who conquers I will grant to eat of the tree of life, which is in the paradise of God."[16] It is an image of eternal life in heaven, a reward for those who have washed their robes and made them white in the blood of the Lamb.[17] With the ending of death, access to the tree of life is restored.

The Gospel of Christ's atonement and forgiveness is made available to all who will receive it, and live into it, by faith. "The Spirit and the Bride say 'Come!' And let him who hears say, 'Come!' Whoever is thirsty, let him come, and whoever wishes, let him take the free gift of the water of life."[18]

It is Jesus who said to the Samaritan woman at the well, "whoever drinks the water I give him will never thirst. Indeed, the water I give him will become in him a spring of water welling up to eternal life."[19]

This is the coinage of fulfillment, of personal satisfaction – the slaking of thirst – the realization that one need never thirst again, that desire is constantly consummated. The bank will never be in deficit. We can draw on all the credit of the Son of God to cover our needs. It is the experience of having arrived and being able to relax. It is the end of the journey. As John Newton, the former sailor, put it in his hymn:

"Through many dangers, toils and snares,
I have already come;
'Tis grace hath brought me safe thus far,
And grace will lead me home."

When we've been there ten thousand years,
Bright shining as the sun,
We've no less days to sing God's praise
Than when we'd first begun."

Where is this land of life everlasting? It is in another dimension. It is a new heaven and a new earth where "the former things will not be remembered, nor will they come to mind."[20] All the painful memories will be erased for those who are cleansed in the blood of the Lamb, and whose names are in the Lamb's book of life.

I began this book with a prayer by Eric Milner-White. It is fitting to close it with his affirmation on the words of St. Augustine: "God is the country of the soul."

THE COUNTRY

"No longer is the country of God far off;
    faith is nearing sight,
        and the long search, possession.
Yet even there we shall continue seeking,
    so wonderful, so inexhaustible it is;
A country beyond storm or change,
    where rest is complete, but always awake,
        active upon a Father's miracles of good;
    where light illumines love, and love dazzles light,
    where righteousness and peace kiss each other;
    where there are no more shames,
        and no more tears.

You are yourself, O God, that country,
        you are Eden everlasting;
    yourself the tree of healing for all mankind,
    yourself the river of our cleansing,
    yourself the slaking of our thirst,
        yourself full truth and perfect knowledge
GOD HIMSELF, the country of my soul;
    you are my beginning before I was born,
        my end without an end.

God bring me to this country!
    God help me by the hand,
    God clothe me with his grace,
    God fold me in his life,
        for evermore."[21]

EPILOGUE

When I walk on the beach, some mornings I see a strange vessel anchored in the Atlantic Ocean. It is the "Polly L," built by Doug Pope, Arnie Hoflander, and Ed Gavron, as a research and recovery vessel to find shipwrecks. Their treasure hunting company, Amelia Research and Recovery, deploys new lift boat technologies to locate, study, and salvage treasures in ocean sites. They are currently working on the rediscovery of the *Santa Margarita*, a known treasure shipwreck first discovered by Mel Fisher in 1980. Jim Sinclair, the consulting project archeologist writes that "evidence is mounting, we are closing in on fabulous new discoveries. Compelling new findings are the result of Amelia's work." It is believed that two 1715 Spanish fleet vessels, the *San Miguel* and the *Ciervo* are wrecked near the south end of Amelia Island.

Amelia's senior management and consultants have decades of experience in shipwreck exploration and salvage. Their full time project managers, ship's captains, dive masters, operational and administrative support staff are experienced and dedicated. They believe that with their expertise they can locate and recover the treasure they are seeking. I certainly wish them well on their search.

If such effort is expended in finding such buried treasures in the sands of the Atlantic Ocean, why not expend comparable effort in recovering the mysteries of faith. God has put into our hearts the desire for us to seek him and reach out for him and find him. He is not far from each one of us.[1] But it does require us to act on this desire. It does require us to seek, and to reach out. That is why we read, and study, and discuss with one another the truth of faith. That is why we go to church, and hear sermons, and attend classes. If only we had a portion of the interest, the curiosity, the energy of those who seek for buried treasure in the ocean. If we did, we would find our efforts richly rewarded. The sea of God's truth will yield up its secrets, and we will be enriched beyond measure. God is no man's debtor. He rewards those who earnestly seek him.[2]

ENDNOTES

PREFACE
[1] Soren Kierkegaard, *Training in Christianity*, trans. by Walter Lowrie (Princeton, 1947), 260

INTRODUCTION – DISCOVERING A TREASURE SHIP
[1] Gary Kinder, *Ship of Gold*, (New York, Vintage, 1999) 182
[2] Hebrews 11:1
[3] Kinder, op.cit., 452, 453
[4] Kinder, op.cit., 482
[5] Ephesians 3:8
[6] Romans 10:8
[7] Kinder, op.cit., 50

PART ONE – SEEKING THE TREASURE
[1] C.S. Lewis, *Mere Christianity*, Fontana, Collins, London, 1960), 131

CHAPTER 1   DOUBTING THOMAS
[1] Kinder, op.cit., 87
[2] John 20:25
[3] Matthew 11:28-30
[4] Paul Vitz, *Faith of the Fatherless: The Psychology of Atheism* (Dallas, Spence, 1999), quoted by Lynn Anderson, *If I Really Believe, Why Do I Have These Doubts?* (Howard, 2000), 26,27
[5] Anderson, op.cit., 29,30
[6] Henri J. Nouwen, *Reaching Out* (New York, Doubleday, 1957), 127
[7] Nouwen, op.cit.,128
[8] John 20:24-29

CHAPTER 2   TURNING DOUBT TO GOOD
[1] Mark 9:22-24
[2] Gary E. Parker, *The Gift of Doubt: From crisis to authentic faith* (Harper & Row, San Francisco, 1990), 62
[3] Parker, op.cit., 64
[4] Robert Schuller, *Tough Times Never Last, but Tough People Do* (New York: Thomas Nelson, 1983), 25-28) quoted by Parker.
[5] Parker, op.cit., 71
[6] Herbert Williams, *No Room for Doubt* (Nashville: Broadman Press, 1976), 1:183, quoted by Parker
[7] 1 Peter 3:15
[8] Parker, op.cit., 75

CHAPTER 3   REASONABLE DOUBT
[1] Anderson, op.cit., 37-48
[2] John R. W. Stott, *Your Mind Matters* (Downers Grove, Inter-Varsity Press, 1972), 10
[3] Stott, op.cit. 34
[4] Joshua 24:15
[5] 1 Corinthians 1:19,20
[6] Frederick Buechner, *The Magnificent Defeat* (New York: Seabury, 1983), 47 quoted by Anderson, op.cit., 45
[7] John 12:37,39
[8] Buechner, op. cit., 48

CHAPTER 4   A WORKING DEFINITION OF FAITH
[1] Parker, op. cit., 77
[2] 2 Timothy 2:11,13
[3] Hebrews 11:1-3
[4] Dr. Armand M. Nicholi, Jr., *The Question of God* (New York, The Free Press, 2002), 36
[5] Soren Kierkegaard, *The Last Years: Journals 1853-1855*, edited and translated by Ronald Gregor Smith (New York, Harper & Row, 1965), 154,155
[6] Clark Pinnock, *A Case for Faith*, 13, q.v. Gary E. Parker, op.cit.,

CHAPTER 5   THE RISK OF FAITH
[1] Romans 4:16-18
[2] Joshua 24:2
[3] E.M. Blaiklock, *Today's Handbook of Bible Characters*, (Minneapolis, Bethany, 1979), 18
[4] Genesis 12:1-3
[5] Genesis 17:17
[6] Romans 4:19-21
[7] Hebrews 11:13,16

CHAPTER 6   STAGES OF FAITH
[1] 2 Thessalonians 1:3
[2] William Shakespeare, *As You Like It*, II, vii, 139
[3] John Westerhoff, *Will Our Children Have Faith?* (New York, Seabury, 1976), 89-101
[4] 2 Timothy 1:5,6
[5] 1 Peter 2:2
[6] Anderson, op.cit., 86
[7] James 1:6-8
[8] Anderson, op.cit.,87
[9] 1 Timothy 3:7
[10] 2 Timothy 1:12

[11] Hebrews 5:12
[12] Janet O. Hagberg, Robert A. Guelich, *The Critical Journey: Stages in the Life of Faith* (Dallas, Word, 1989), 12
[13] For a full description of this stage see Hagberg and Guelich, op.cit., chapter 7, *The Wall*, 114-130
[14] Mark 10:15

CHAPTER 7   QUESTIONING FAITH

[1] New and Selected Poems, 1956-1996 (University of Arkansas Press, 1996)
[2] Parker, op. cit., 121
[3] Isaiah 55:9
[4] Job 42:3
[5] Parker, op.cit., 122
[6] Parker, op.cit., 123-125
[7] John Stott, *The Cross of Christ* (InterVarsity Press, Downers Grove, Illinois, 1986), 336,337

CHAPTER 8   CHOOSING FAITH

[1] John 7:17
[2] Anderson, op.cit., 114
[3] Anderson, op. cit., 100
[4] Hebrews 11:6
[5] 1 John 2:17
[6] Anderson, op.cit., 108
[7] Matthew 7:21-23
[8] Dietrich Bonhoeffer, *Letters and Papers From Prison*, ed. Eberhard Bethge (Touchstone, New York, 1997) 8,9
[9] Helmut Thielecke, *How To Believe Again* (Philadephia, Fortress, 1972), 17
[10] *Eighteen Upbuilding Discourses*, ed. & trans. Howard V. Hong and Edna H. Hong (Princeton University Press, 1990), 347-375

CHAPTER 9   THE SUBJECTIVITY OF FAITH

[1] Roger Poole, *Towards Deep Subjectivity* (Harper, New York, 1972), 44-48
[2] Donald M. Mackay, *The Clockwork Image* (Inter-Varsity, London, 1974), 43
[3] Poole, op.cit., 120
[4] Poole, op.cit., 121
[5] Luke 11:29-32
[6] Luke 11:33-36
[7] 1 Corinthians 2:14
[8] John 9:39-41

CHAPTER 10   FAITH HAS ITS REASONS
[1] John 1:43-51
[2] John 1:29
[3] Eugene Peterson, *The Message* (NavPress, Colorado Springs, 1993), 187
[4] Daniel Taylor, *The Myth of Certainty* (InterVarsity Press, Downers Grove, Illinois, 1992), 70,71
[5] Taylor, op.cit., 25
[6] Soren Kierkegaard, *The Point of View of My Work As an Author*
[7] Matthew 24:24

CHAPTER 11   THE GIFT OF FAITH
[1] New York Times Book Review, September 5, 2004, 19
[2] Murray A. Rae, *Kierkegaard's Vision of the Incarnation: By Faith Transformed* (Clarendon Press, Oxford, 1997)
[3] Matthew 13:14
[4] Rae, op.cit., 93
[5] Matthew 16:17
[6] Luke 18:9-14
[7] Rae, op.cit., 160,161
[8] Romans 12:2
[9] John 3:3-8
[10] Ephesians 2:1-11
[11] Rae, op.cit., 16,17
[12] Romans 10:14-17
[13] Rae, op.cit., 159
[14] Rae, op.cit., 2
[15] Rae, op.cit., 68

CHAPTER 12   WHY I BELIEVE IN JESUS CHRIST
[1] Acts 17:25,28
[2] Romans 11:36
[3] 1 Corinthians 8:6
[4] John 1:1-4,14
[5] Ecclesiastes 3:11
[6] John 11:25
[7] Romans 3:19,23
[8] Romans 7:15-19
[9] Revelation 3:20
[10] Matthew 25:35,36
[11] Ephesians 2:14

[12] Matthew 28:20
[13] Philippians 4:13
[14] Philippians 3:10,11
[15] Hebrews 12:2
[16] Matthew 11:29

PART TWO – THE TREASURES OF FAITH

CHAPTER 13   I BELIEVE
[1] Romans 10:9; 1 Corinthians 12:3; 2 Corinthians 4:5; Philippians 2:11
[2] The following is a summary from Alister McGrath, *I Believe* (Zondervan, Grand Rapids, 1991), 14-16
[3] *The Message*, 275

CHAPTER 14   GOD THE FATHER ALMIGHTY
[1] Klyne Snodgrass, *Ephesians, The NIV Application Commentary*, Zondervan, Grand Rapids, 1996), 185,186
[2] Isaiah 49:15
[3] Isaiah 66:13
[4] John 14:5-14
[5] Ephesians 3:14,15
[6] Romans 8:15,16
[7] John Stott, *God's New Society* (Inter-Varsity Press, Leicester, England, 1979), 134
[8] Helmut Thielecke, *The Waiting Father* (Harper & Row, New York, 1959), 29
[9] Howard Edington, *The Forgotten Man of Christmas* (Synchronicity Press, Sanford, 2000), 54
[10] 1 John 3:1
[11] John 1:12,13
[12] Ephesians 3:16-21
[13] Luke 11:11-13

CHAPTER 15   MAKER OF HEAVEN AND EARTH
[1] Hebrews 11:3
[2] J.B. Phillips, *The New Testament in Modern English* (Geoffrey Bles, London, 1960), 470
[3] Stephen Hawking, *A Brief History of Time* (Bantam, 1988),141
[4] John Polkinghorne, *The Faith of a Physicist* (Princeton, New Jersey, 1994), 73
[5] Genesis 1:31
[6] William Barclay, *The Apostles' Creed* (Westminster John Knox, Louisville, 1998), 38-43
[7] 1 Timothy 4:4

[8] C.E.B. Cranfield, *The Apostles' Creed* (Eerdmans, Grand Rapids, 1993), 17,18
[9] Kenneth Miller, *Brown Alumni Magazine*, Volume 100, No.2, November/December 1999, article: *Finding Darwin's God: A Scientist's Search for Common Ground Between God and Evolution*, 37-43
[10] McGrath, op.cit., 41,42
[11] Acts 17:28
[12] 2 Corinthians 5:17

CHAPTER 16   JESUS CHRIST
[1] A.V.G. Allen, *Life of Phillips Brooks*, ii,340-342
[2] Acts 3:6
[3] Acts 3:16
[4] Matthew 1:21
[5] Malcolm Muggeridge, *The End of Christendom*, (Eerdmans, Grand Rapids, 1980), 56
[6] Ephesians 3:8

CHAPTER 17   HIS ONLY SON
[1] John 5:19
[2] William Barclay, *The Gospel of John* (Westminster, Philadelphia, 1975), i, 188
[3] John 5:20
[4] Barclay, ibid.
[5] John 5:21-23
[6] Matthew 21:41
[7] John 5:25-27
[8] William Barclay, *The Gospel of John* (Westminster, Philadelphia, 1975), I, 189,190
[9] John 5:18
[10] Barclay, op.cit., 187
[11] Luke 9:35
[12] Hebrews 2:11
[13] Romans 8:31,32
[14] John Calvin, *Romans* (Constable, Edinburgh, 1893), 322,333

CHAPTER 18   OUR LORD
[1] Luke 7:6-8
[2] Peterson, op.cit, 414
[3] Matthew 11:29
[4] 2 Corinthians 10:5
[5] Dietrich Bonhoeffer, *The Cost of Discipleship* (SCM, London, 1948), 31
[6] Luke Timothy Johnson, *The Creed* (Doubleday, New York, 2003), 118

[7] Philippians 2:9-11
[8] John Stott, *The Contemporary Christian* (InterVarsity Press, Downers Grove, Illinois, 1992), 98

CHAPTER 19   CONCEIVED - BORN
[1] Luke 1:35,37
[2] J. I. Packer, *The Apostles' Creed* (Tyndale, Wheaton, 1985), 44,45

CHAPTER 20   SUFFERED UNDER PILATE
[1] Article, *Pilate*, by D.H. Wheaton, *The New Bible Dictionary*, ed. J.D. Douglas (InterVarsity, London, 1962), 997
[2] Alister McGrath, *I Believe* (Zondervan, Grand Rapids, 1991), 71
[3] Alister McGrath, ibid.
[4] Acts 2:23
[5] Acts 3:13,14
[6] Colossians 1:24
[7] 2 Corinthians 1:5; Philippians 3:10
[8] Drawn from articles in *Christianity Today*, March 2003, and *Episcopal Life*, March 2003.
[9] The Office of International Religious Freedom, www.state.gov/g/drl/irf/.
Amnesty International, www.amnestyusa.org
The Barnabas Fund, www.barnabasfund.org.
The Voice of the Martyrs, www.persecution.com
Institute on Religion and Democracy, www.ird-renew.org/liberty
Compass Direct, www.compassdirect.org.
[10] McGrath, op.cit. 72
[11] Isaiah 53:3

CHAPTER 21   CRUCIFIED, DEAD AND BURIED
[1] Hebrews 9:14,15,28
[2] Romans 5:8
[3] 2 Corinthians 5:15
[4] 1 John 3:16; 4:10
[5] Charles Cranfield, *The Apostles' Creed*, 33
[6] Kenneth Cragg; in M. Kamel Hussein, City of Wrong, tr. Kenneth Cragg (Amsterdam: Djambatan, 1959), xi
[7] John Stott, *The Cross of Christ* (InterVarsity, Downers Grove, 1986), 258
[8] Colin Chapman, *Christianity on Trial* (Tyndale, Wheaton, 1975), 501f., citing Hebrews 2:14
[9] John Stott, op.cit., 42
[10] Alister McGrath, *I Believe*, 83

CHAPTER 22   DESCENDED TO THE DEAD
[1] John Calvin, *Institutes of the Christian Religion*, trans. Ford Lewis Battles, ed. John T. McNeill (Philadelphia, Westminster, 1960), 1:513
[2] J.I. Packer, *The Apostles' Creed*, 54
[3] Matthew 10:28, see also 2 Cor.5:1-5
[4] John Pearson, *An Exposition of the Creed*, 1847, 356,357
[5] Acts 2:27
[6] Acts 2:31
[7] *The Apostles' Creed*, 108
[8] *The Gospel of the Hereafter*, 61,62
[9] Calvin, op.cit., 1:516
[10] James F. Kay in *Exploring & Proclaiming the Apostles' Creed*, ed. Roger E. Van Harn (Eerdmans, Grand Rapids, 2004), 125
[11] Kay, op.cit., 127,128
[12] quoted in W.H. Griffith Thomas, *The Principles of Theology*, 71,72
[13] Hebrews 2:14

CHAPTER 23   HE ROSE FROM THE DEAD
[1] James 4:14
[2] Ezekiel 37:11-13
[3] 1 Corinthians 15:3-8
[4] Luke Timothy Johnson, op.cit., 180
[5] Romans 10:9
[6] Romans 8;11
[7] Daniel 12:2,3
[8] John 11:25
[9] John 8:12

CHAPTER 24   HE ASCENDED INTO HEAVEN
[1] Bernard of Clairvaux (1090-1153), *On the Christian Year*, tans. By a Religious from CSMV
[2] Acts 1:9-11
[3] John 20:17
[4] Exodus 24:16,17; 40:34)
[5] Luke 9:34,35
[6] John 14:2
[7] Hebrews 6:19,20
[8] John 3:13
[9] C. S. Lewis, *Mere Christianity*, 143-145
[10] Luke 23:43
[11] Ruth Etchells, *Just As I Am: Personal prayers for every day* (Triangle, SPCK, London, 1994), 151

Endnotes

CHAPTER 25   SEATED AT THE RIGHT HAND
[1] Acts 2:33
[2] Acts 5:31
[3] Acts 7:56
[4] Matthew 26:64
[5] Romans 8:34
[6] Colossians 2:15
[7] Romans 8:37
[8] Ephesians 1:19,20; 2:6
[9] Colossians 3:1
[10] Matthew 25:31-33
[11] Romans 1:16

CHAPTER 26   COME TO JUDGE
[1] Acts 10:42
[2] Acts 17:31
[3] 2 Corinthians 5:10
[4] John Pearson, *An Exposition of the Creed* (Henry Washbourne, London, 1847), 442
[5] Romans 2:16
[6] Pearson, op.cit., 458
[7] John 5:24
[8] McGrath, op.cit., 103-105
[9] Psalm 139:1-4
[10] Roy Angell, *Shields of Brass* (Broadman, Nashville, 1965), 109,110

CHAPTER 27   THE HOLY SPIRIT
[1] Michael Green, *Adventure of Faith* (Zondervan, Grand Rapids, 2001), 369
[2] Galatians 5:25
[3] Luke 11:13
[4] Peterson, *The Message*, Acts 2:2-4, 240
[5] Genesis 1:2; 2:7
[6] John 3:8
[7] Exodus 14:21
[8] Ezekiel 37:9,10
[9] Mary Ellen Ashcroft, *Dogspell* (Forest of Peace, Leavenworth, 2000), 75-78
[10] Acts 7:51
[11] Ephesians 3:16, Romans 15:13

CHAPTER 28   THE HOLY, CATHOLIC CHURCH
[1] 1 Peter 2:9
[2] Peterson, op.cit., 289
[3] Matthew 16:18

CHAPTER 29   THE COMMUNION OF SAINTS
[1] Hebrew 11:32-40
[2] Hebrews 12:22-24
[3] 1 Thessalonians 4:13,14
[4] William Barclay, *A Barclay Prayer Book* (SCM, London, 1990), 176,177

CHAPTER 30   THE FORGIVENESS OF SINS
[1] Matthew 18:23-25
[2] Matthew 18:28-30
[3] Luke 11:4, 1 John 1:9
[4] Charles L. Allen, *When The Heart is Hungry* (Revell, Westwood, N.J., 1955), 88,89
[5] Romans 12:19

CHAPTER 31   RESURRECTION OF THE BODY
[1] Ray S. Anderson, *On Being Human: The Creaturely Saga of the Creaturely Soul* in *What Happened to the Soul?* ed. Warren S. Brown, Nancey Murphy & H. Newton Malony (Fortress, Minneapolis, 1998), 189
[2] Psalm 139:13-16
[3] Peterson, *The Message*, 374 (2 Corinthians 5:1-10)
[4] 1 Corinthians 15:53,54
[5] 1 Corinthians 15:42-44
[6] Job 19:26,27
[7] Romans 8:11; cf. 1 Thessalonians 4:13-15
[8] Oscar Cullmann, *Immortality of the Soul or Resurrection of the Dead?* (Epworth, London, 1958), 37
[9] Ibid.
[10] Romans 8:22-24
[11] Cullmann, op.cit., 38,39,59,60
[12] William H. Willimon, *Pulpit Resource*, Vol. 31, No. 2, 21-23

CHAPTER 32   THE LIFE EVERLASTING
[1] Malcolm Muggeridge, *Confessions of a Twentieth-Century Pilgrim* (Harper, San Francisco, 1988), 145,146
[2] Op. cit., 147,148
[3] Op. cit., 148,150
[4] John 4:14
[5] John 3:16
[6] John 6:54,57

[7] Revelation 21:2,4
[8] Revelation 21:27
[9] Revelation 22:2,3
[10] Revelation 21:24,25
[11] Revelation 7:9
[12] 1 Thessalonians 4:17
[13] 1 Corinthians 13:9-12
[14] Romans 8:38
[15] Penelope Fitzgerald, *The Knox Brothers* (Counterpoint, Washington, D.C., 2000), 262
[16] Revelation 2:7
[17] Revelation 22:14
[18] Revelation 22:17
[19] John 4:14
[20] Isaiah 65:17
[21] Eric Milner-White, *My God My Glory* (Triangle, London, 1994), 213

EPILOGUE
[1] Acts 17:27
[2] Hebrews 11:6

ACKNOWLEDGEMENTS

This book grew out of a series of sermons I gave at Amelia Plantation Chapel. I want to thank the Chapel Board: Bill Gower, Sandy Shaw, Joe Marasco, Rose Rigdon, Dave Smith, Norm Purdue, Jan Davis, Carol Gentry, and Jimmy Jones for their generous support and encouragement. I am grateful to my secretary, Mary Thweatt, and Ellen Wilson for their indefatigable proofing.

I gratefully acknowledge permission to reproduce copyright material. Every effort has been made to trace and acknowledge copyright holders. I apologize for any errors or omissions that may remain, and would ask those concerned to contact the publishers, who will ensure that full acknowledgement with be made in the future.

Excerpts from *Mere Christianity* are reprinted by permission of C.S. Lewis Pte. Ltd. 1942,1943,1944,1952; from *Kierkegaard's Vision of the Incarnation: By Faith Transformed* by permission of Oxford University Press; from *What Happened to the Soul*, by permission of Augsburg Fortress; from *NIV Application Commentary*, and *I Believe*, by permission of Zondervan; from *New and Selected Poems, 1956-1996*, by permission of University of Arkansas Press; from *The Creed*, by permission of Doubleday; from *Dogspell*, by permission of Ave Maria Press; from *The Myth of Certainty*, and the works of John Stott, by permission of InterVarsity Press; from *Pulpit Resource*, by permission of Logos Productions, Inc.; from *The Apostles' Creed* and *Christianity on Trial*, by permission of Tyndale House Publishers, Inc.; from the works of William Barclay, by permission of Westminster John Knox Press; from *If I Really Believe, Why Do I Have These Doubts?* by permission of Howard Publishing Company; from *My God, My*

John Knox Press; from *If I Really Believe, Why Do I Have These Doubts?* by permission of Howard Publishing Company; from *My God, My Glory*, by permission of the Friends of York Minster; from *The Knox Brothers*, by permission of The Perseus Books Group; from *Ship of Gold in the Deep Blue Sea*, by permission of Grove/Atlantic, Inc.; from *The Faith of a Physicist*, by permission of Princeton University Press; Ascension Day prayer from *Just As I Am*, by permission of Dr D. Ruth Etchells; from *The Gift of Doubt*, by permission of Dr. Gary Parker.

As always, I pay tribute to the unflagging support and encouragement of my wife, Antoinette, who is the perfect literary companion, amongst her many other virtues.

A NOTE ABOUT THE AUTHOR

Ted Schroder was born in 1941, in Hokitika, New Zealand, and has lived in the United States since 1971. He was educated at Canterbury University, Christchurch, New Zealand, and Cranmer Hall, St. John's College, in the University of Durham. Ordained in St. Paul's Cathedral, London to be the Assistant Curate of All Souls, Langham Place, he became Chaplain of the Polytechnic of Central London (now University of Westminster). After moving across the Atlantic he assumed the position of Dean of the Chapel at Gordon College, Massachusetts, and assistant minister at Christ Church of Hamilton-Wenham. In 1976 he moved to Jacksonville, Florida, where he served on the staff of the Bishop, and then pastored Grace Church, Orange Park. From 1986 he was Rector of Christ Church, San Antonio, Texas, until 2000 when he took up his present post at Amelia Plantation Chapel on Amelia Island, Florida. He serves on the Board of Trustees of Trinity Episcopal School for Ministry, Ambridge, Pennsylvania, and is also President of the Board of Directors of Sutton Place Behavioral Health, which provides mental health and addiction services in Nassau County. He has been married to Antoinette, a South Carolina native and Bronte scholar, since 1970, and they have two daughters, and three grandchildren.

PRAISE FOR *INWARD LIGHT*

"Christians who value honesty and have a feeling for things around them will find these broodings bracing and refreshing."
James I. Packer
author of *Knowing God*

"Having valued Ted Schroder's friendship for nearly forty years, I am delighted that his book has been published. Although its two parts are in many ways different from each other, both are the product of profound understanding of the human heart, and prolonged reflection. Ted's keen observation and vivid style enables his readers to see what he sees, hear from he hears and so feel what he feels."
John Stott,
author of *Basic Christianity*

"It's a privilege to call Ted Schroder my friend. We've served, eaten, and prayed together many times. My prayer is that you, through these pages will discover what I've found in fellowship: Ted has a great heart, good word, and genuine faith."
Max Lucado